MOZART'S EUROPE

The Early Journeys

MOZART'S FIRST EFFORTS AT COMPOSITION.

Iwo and Pamela Załuski

The Book Guild Ltd.
Sussex, England

The Book Guild Ltd.
25 High Street,
Lewes, Sussex

First published 1993

Set in Baskerville
Typesetting by Kudos Graphics
Slinfold, Horsham, West Sussex

Printed in Great Britain by
Antony Rowe Ltd.
Chippenham, Wiltshire.

A catalogue record for this book is
available from the British Library

ISBN 0 86332 737 0

CONTENTS

ACT THREE

ACT FOUR

ACT FIVE

LIST OF ILLUSTRATIONS

LIST OF MAPS

Map extracts are taken from an original post route map, circa 1760

PREFACE

'People who do not travel are indeed miserable creatures,' wrote Wolfgang Amadeus Mozart, 'A fellow of mediocre talent will remain a mediocrity whether he travels or not, but one of superior talent will go to seed if he remains in the same place.'

Mozart had been exposed to the European experience since he was six, thanks entirely to his father, Leopold, who originally fostered in his brilliant son the love of travel that was to stay with him till his death.

In the eighteenth century, Europe was riven with strife as much as in any other century: it was fortunate for Mozart that during the years of his travels, between 1763 and 1791, Europe was relatively peaceful and travel was not only possible, but also fashionable.

The Age of Enlightenment had arrived, and had spawned enquiring and open minds, curious about distant lands, foreign customs and different cultures. Many travellers chose to chronicle their experiences and impressions, thus bringing to life the rich and varied European milieu in which the Mozart journeys were set.

Among the great chronicler-travellers of the latter part of the eighteenth century was Leopold Mozart himself – cultured, urbane, enquiring, often intolerant to the point of bigotry; through his letters to his friend and landlord, Lorenz Hagenauer, we glean a sharp, if sometimes one-sided, insight into the overall Mozart story.

The picture of eighteenth century Europe is further enhanced by the writings of other contemporary travellers, such as the musicologist Dr Charles Burney, the

The house in Getreidegasse, Salzburg where Mozart was born.

Source: unknown.

witty and often cutting correspondent Horace Walpole, the meticulous naturalist Thomas Pennant, music publisher and Mozart pilgrim Vincent Novello and his wife Mary, as well as Vincent Novello's friend and pupil, the musician Edward Holmes.

Fired by this wealth of written word, as well as by an all-consuming love of Mozart's music, we embarked (with the help of a good road map of Europe circa 1760) on our own Mozart Odyssey in search of ghosts, retracing the Mozart journeys, and comparing our experiences on the roads – and waterways – of Europe with those of our predecessors of the eighteenth and nineteenth centuries.

In this book we have sought not only to tell the stories of Mozart's journeys, but also to set them within the essential European framework, both from a contemporary and a modern point of view, drawing on the many analogies that still exist across the centuries.

Although our odyssey was personal, our primary aim in writing this book has been to reconstruct these journeys as accurately as possible; to list as many of the sites as it is possible to discover in both published document and archive, and to plot the actual routes.

The map extracts shown in each Act are taken from an original map of the post routes of the German Empire, printed in Amsterdam, circa 1760. Leopold Mozart would have used a similar map to plan their journeys.

Many of the buildings and the post stages may no longer be there.

But the ghosts are.

Iwo & Pamela Załuski

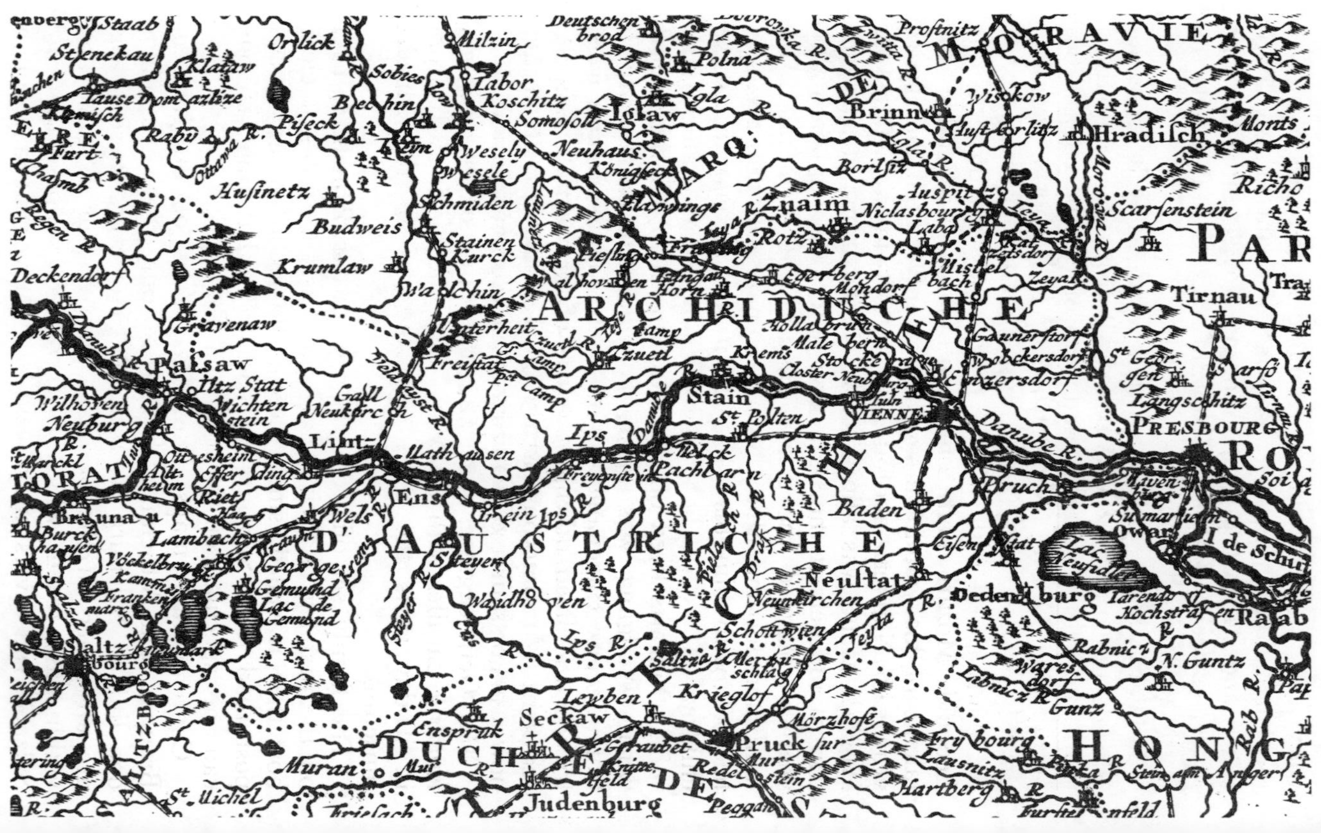
MORAVIE
ARCHIDUCHE
D'AUSTRICHE
HONG
DUCH
PAR
Danube R.
PRESBOURG
VIENNE
Tirnau
Budweis
Krumlaw
Passaw
Lintz
Ens
Stain
St Polten
Baden
Neustat
Judenburg
Znaim
Brinn
Iglaw
Neuhaus
Hradisch
Lac Neusidler
Dedenburg
Pruck sur Mur
Seckaw
Leuben
Saltzbourg
Husinetz

OVERTURE

Leopold Mozart had ambitious plans to promote the talents of his young family. Having already taken eleven year old Nannerl and the six year old Wolfgang, or Wolferl, as he was affectionately called, on a three week trip to Munich at the beginning of 1762, later on in that year he planned the second journey of their quest for fame and fortune, this time to Vienna. On this occasion he took with him his wife, Maria Anna, as well as the children.

The Mozarts lived on the third floor of 9 Getreidegasse, where Wolfgang was born. They rented an apartment from Lorenz Hagenauer, the Mozarts' landlord and good friend, who lived downstairs with his family. He was the recipient of numerous letters from Leopold, which are now a major source of documentation of their journeys.

The Getreidegasse is on the south side of the Salzach, running parallel with the river, and one block away from it. Today it is the most important of all the Mozart museums.

The family set off from their home on September 18th on the first leg of their journey to Passau. It is not clear how they travelled, since there is no record of an official post road from Salzburg to Passau at that time, so one can only speculate on the route that they took.

Contemporary maps show the towns of Burghausen, Braunau and Altheim, although the only road is a minor one linking Salzburg to Braunau. However, these towns are all either on the Salzach–Inn river, or at any rate, within easy reach, which leads one to suppose that the Salzach–Inn rivers may well have served as a through route to Passau.

The River Salzach rises in the Alps and flows northwards through Salzburg to join the Inn, which in turn joins the Danube at Passau. A great deal of travel was done by river and canal in the eighteenth century, and it is possible that they went by boat, since the Mozarts did not own a carriage at that time. Grein, situated on the Danube about half way between Passau and Vienna, is a pleasant town dominated by the Greinburg, a schloss[1] built in 1493, now containing a museum of Danube Navigation. It furnishes some fascinating insights into conditions under which the Mozarts travelled that year.

The argument against the river route is that Leopold made no mention of a river trip to Passau: in fact he made no mention whatsoever of the first leg of this trip, which would lead one to suppose that they most probably went by road.

Mozart covered the Salzburg–Vienna route several times, on most occasions taking the direct route by way of Linz and St Pölten. On this particular journey the river trip between Passau and Vienna is documented, and today it is still possible to go from Passau to Vienna by boat.

The eighteenth century road from Salzburg to Passau is by no means clear, but the most likely route would be to Braunau by way of Mattighofen, and thence to Passau on the Austrian side of the River, passing through Altheim and Schärding. This road runs along the River Salzach, which serves as the Austro–German frontier all the way to Passau, as indeed it did in 1762.

It took the Mozarts two days to reach Passau, and they arrived there at five o'clock in the afternoon of September 20th, and put up at Zum Roten Krebs. The building, restored and renovated since, is now the hotel Zum Grauen Hasen, situated in 1 Oberer Sand.

In Passau the Mozarts were delayed by the recently appointed Prince-Bishop of Passau, Josef Maria von Thun, who engaged Wolferl to play before him, but kept the Mozarts waiting for five days. When the boy finally

[1]Schloss – a castle.

performed at the Residenz, he was paid the princely sum of one ducat, which annoyed Leopold, who ended up out of pocket. Besides, the delay had caused the Mozarts to miss out on an opportunity to play at a concert in Linz. Leopold's subsequent thoughts about the Bishop were not very charitable.

In June of the following year, in a letter to Lorenz Hagenauer, Leopold wrote that 'the Bishop of Passau is dead. Requiescat in pace. Judicia Dei. God can settle many an account at a stroke.' Leopold possessed a deep conviction that God was always on his side!

The magnificent and awesomely spacious Cathedral of St Stephen stands majestically at the highest point of the old town of Passau, and boasts the biggest church organ in the world, since its repair and restoration in 1928. The original Baroque outer casing was built in 1731 by J. M. Gotz, and since its restoration the action has been further renovated in 1980 by Messrs Eisenbarth, of Passau.

It is doubtful whether little Wolferl played on the original organ, although, with five days to kill, no doubt his father took him to see the Cathedral and its organ. Leopold always made a point of taking Wolfgang to see and hear organs wherever possible, which may be why Mozart loved the organ so much, and said later that, 'to my eyes and ears the organ is the king of all instruments'.

In the nave there are three episcopal memorials. On the crossing columns, left, there is one of Prince-Bishop von Thun. The Neue Residenz, where Mozart performed for the Bishop, adjoins the Cathedral, and is where the Prince-Bishops of Passau lived and officiated. On the first floor hangs a portrait bearing the inscription, 'Fürstbischof Joseph Maria Graf von Thun-Hohenstein 1761–63'.

One church that the family did visit was the Pilgrimage Church of Mariahilf, situated high up on the Mariahilfberg. Lorenz Hagenauer had requested that they visit the church, and Nannerl had promised him that they would: consequently, the Mozarts all went to the church and said a prayer for him.

After Passau, the Danube becomes the border, at any rate as far as Engelhartszell. The old post road linking Passau to Linz, used by Mozart on his Frankfurt journey in 1790, is now route 130 on the Austrian side of the river. It is perhaps the most beautiful stretch of road on the whole journey. Known as the Upper Danube Valley, it follows the contours of the river among wooded hills scattered with enchanting vistas of Bavarian towns, villages, and the occasional hilltop schloss on the other side.

Just beyond Hilkering the road splits, with the post road going into Linz through Eferding and Wilhering.

The Mozarts left Passau on September 26th by 'ordinary' boat, an economical form of river travel, and docked in Linz that same evening at five o'clock. They put up at Zur Dreifaltigkeit in Hofgasse 14, a lodging house run by two spinster sisters by the name of Kiener, who doted on the two children and spoiled them disgracefully! Today, the site is at Hofburg 11, which is a cafe. A plaque commemorates the Mozarts' stay in 1762.

It was in this city that chance played a significant part in the Mozart fortunes. A certain Countess Schlick had heard the Mozarts performing, and had been won over by Wolfgang's extraordinary talent. By coincidence the Hungarian Chancellor, Count Nikolaus Palffy, had called on the Countess while passing through Linz. She persuaded him to linger long enough to hear the Mozart children playing at a concert held at the inn. The Count agreed, and was impressed enough to enthuse later on about the amazing six year old boy to the Archduke Joseph at Schönbrunn, who in turn mentioned him to his mother, the Empress Maria Theresia. As a direct result, she commanded that the Mozarts should present themselves at the Imperial Court on their arrival in Vienna.

The city centre of Linz is situated largely on the south bank, where the Danube is spanned by the Niebelungenbrücke. Directly opposite the south end of this bridge is the Hauptplatz, the gateway to Linz's historic centre. On the Promenade, opposite the Landes Theater, is the Tourist Office. This building used to belong to the Linz branch of the ubiquitous House of Thun, which played such a significant part in Mozart's life. Mozart wrote the Linz Symphony there, on the first floor, in five days, during a visit to Count Thun in 1783.

On the afternoon of October 4th, the Mozarts continued their journey till they reached the small town of Mauthausen on the north bank of the Danube after dark, and spent the night there.

The following day the Mozarts continued down the river in the company of three monks – two Minorites and a Benedictine. At midday, they stopped at Ybbs for lunch, and visited the Franciscan monastery, where the monks said masses. During these masses Wolferl, at his father's suggestion, played the organ. Consequently, the Franciscan friars, who were entertaining guests to lunch at the time, where so impressed by the sounds coming from the monastery church, that they all, in Leopold's words, 'ran with their guests to the Choir and were nearly struck dead with wonder.'

In 1767, Mozart again visited Ybbs with his parents and Nannerl, and played the organ of the church of St Lawrence, which dominates the town centre. Although deceptively stark from the outside, the interior is sumptuous Austrian baroque. The organ is the original instrument on which Mozart played and the initials 'W.A.M. 1767' are to be found on the casing – accepted evidence of Mozart's visit. It was built in 1725 by Bartholomaus Heinzler, and was repaired and renovated in 1874, and again in 1954.

In 1767 the Mozarts also stopped for lunch at Stift Melk, the magnificent Benedictine Monastery that dominates the town of Melk, downstream from Ybbs. After lunch, Wolferl played the organ at the monastery, and was recognized by the organist.

Stift Melk itself dates back to the eleventh century, although the present superb example of Austrian baroque was inaugurated in 1700 by the Abbot Berthold Dietmayer, and is largely the creation of the architect Jakob Prandtauer of St Pölten.

The Novellos visited Melk twice in the course of their 'Mozart Pilgrimage' in 1829. 'Very handsome church,' wrote Vincent Novello in their travel diaries –

'Roman architecture, particularly rich ornamentation. Handsome organ divided on either side of the window with small choir organ in front and orchestra. Tasteful and appropriate quotation from scripture, *Laudate Dominum cum chordis et organo. laudate, laudate:* A kind of triumphal arch at the extreme of the building just opposite to the grand entrance to the church so that as you come forth from the large doors you see a most beautiful view of the Danube with an old castle and other picturesque objects on both sides of this fine river through this grand archway which is like a magnificent frame for this fine natural landscape. By far the finest convent I have ever seen. Like a princely palace.'

The Emperor's Chambers are now largely a museum, and a celebration of the Benedictine order; it is devoted to Melk's long history. Among its collection of art objects, books and music is a first edition of the *Requiem*, as well as a copy of the Abbé Stadler's book on Mozart. Abbé Maximillian Stadler (1748–1833) was Abbot of Lilienfeld and Kremsmunster, and also a friend and biographer of Mozart.

Further downstream from Melk lies the attractive town of Stein, which is almost a suburb of the larger Krems just beyond it. The Mozarts spent the last night of their river journey there, on October 5th. It consists of the long Landstrasse running parallel to the river, with fortified entrance gates at both ends. It has a number of well maintained old houses, as well as a now de-consecrated Minorite church. This may well have been the destination of the two Minorite monks, at whose masses Wolferl played the organ at Ybbs.

The Rathausplatz in Stein was the birthplace of Ludwig von Köchel (1800–77), who catalogued Mozart's music. One of the squares in the town is named after him.

The following afternoon, October 6th, the Mozarts finally arrived in Vienna, much to everyone's relief. The boat journey had been strenuous and the weather wet and windy, and Wolferl was suffering from a cold.

In Vienna the weather was even worse, with sleet and snow adding more cold and misery to the wind and rain. The Mozarts went through customs, and Wolferl cheered up the officers by playing a merry minuet on his fiddle, the result being that they were ushered through with big smiles and the minimum of fuss.

Leopold took lodgings at a house near the Schwedenbrücke called Zum Weissen Ochsen. The actual house no longer exists, although Fleischmarkt 28, on the corner of Postgasse, in District 1, is recognized as the site.

The Mozarts immediately embarked on a series of concerts in various noble houses, starting on October 9th at the 17th century palace of Count Thomas Vinciguerra Collalto. A contemporary diarist of some considerable repute, Count Karl Zinzendorf, was there. 'At eight o'clock in the evening,' he wrote, 'I collected Lamberg and together we went to Collalto's where Bianchi sang and a little boy who was only five and a half played the clavier.' The Collalto Palace was situated a short distance from St Stephen's Cathedral, in what is now Am Hof 13/Schulhof 8. The palace has since been restored and renovated, although the facade fronting Am Hof dates from 1725. A plaque commemorates Mozart's visit.

During these concerts Leopold himself played the violin, Nannerl played keyboards and sang, while Wolferl played keyboards and, occasionally, the violin. They had their own instruments with them on the trip, including a portable clavier. Their repertoire consisted largely of other peoples' compositions, although Leopold himself was also an adequate composer; as for Wolferl – he had already made a start by now with some minuets and clavier pieces of his own, which were proudly presented on these occasions.

The Mozarts were very much appreciated wherever they played, and everyone was particularly impressed with the friendly and charming little boy, whose finger span was only about a fifth, and whose feet came nowhere near the ground.

On October 11th, the Mozarts visited the Imperial Vice Chancellor, Count Colloredo, and most probably also performed. Among those present were Count Palffy, whom they had already met in Linz, Count Chotek – the

Bohemian Chancellor – and Bishop Esterhazy of the illustrious Hungarian family who employed Haydn. 'All the ladies are in love with my boy,' wrote Leopold. 'We are already of repute here, and when I was alone at the opera on the 10th I heard the Archduke Leopold saying from his box to another on the other side that there was a boy in Vienna who played the clavier marvellously. At eleven o'clock that very same evening I was commanded to go to Schönbrunn.'

Count Zinzendorf recorded further that on October 17th:

> 'I was at the Thuns' where the youngster from Salzburg and his sister played the clavier. The poor little boy plays marvellously. He's a witty child, lively and charming. His sister is a veritable virtuoso. There was much applause.
>
> Fraulein Gudenus, a good clavier player, gave him a kiss, which he wiped from his mouth."

The witty, lively and charming child was evidently no mean judge of character. There are several instances during Wolfgang's childhood of doting women giving him an affectionate kiss, a gesture that he either reciprocated or wiped off with a grimace, as in the case of Fraulein Gudenus.

Perhaps Wolfgang had a sixth sense, whereby he could differentiate between genuine affection and patronizing affectation. He displayed affection to kindly, mothering types of women, while remaining untouched by others.

On October 19th the Mozarts played for the French Ambassador, Comte du Châtelet-Lomont. The latter was evidently most impressed with the Mozarts, because a year later he wrote Leopold a letter of recommendation for the Mozarts' trip to Paris, but Leopold complained that, 'all my letters and recommendations were of no use, even, I'm afraid, that from the French Ambassador in Vienna.'

The highlights, however, were undoubtedly the visits to Schönbrunn to play for the Imperial Family. The first of these took place on October 13th. That was a busy day, for the Mozarts, having performed at Schönbrunn, went on to the Palais Rofrano to perform for Prince von Hildburghausen. The Palais Rofrano later became the

Palais Auersperg; the site today is at Auerspergstrasse 1.

Among the visits to the Imperial Family was one on October 16th, when the children played for the Archdukes Ferdinand, aged eight, and Maximilian, aged five, at the Hofburg.

Both little Archdukes were significant in the Mozart future fortunes: when Wolfgang was fifteen, he was commissioned to write the dramatic serenata, *Ascania in Alba K.111,* for the occasion of the marriage, in 1771, of Archduke Ferdinand to Princess Maria Beatrice di Ricciari of Modena. As for little Maximilian, his lilac suit fitted Wolferl perfectly, as will be revealed in due course!

The concert for the little Archdukes, being obviously very much a childrens' affair, lasted from half past two till half past three. That same evening, the Mozarts had another engagement to play before Count Palffy, this time at his own residence. Today, this site is at Josefplatz 6.

On October 21st, the children performed at Schönbrunn for the last time.

The Imperial Family had taken Wolferl and Nannerl very much to heart, and made the Mozarts feel very welcome. The Empress Maria Theresia, especially, had shown no displeasure when little Wolferl, having played to her for the very first time, jumped up onto her lap and gave her a big kiss. As the Empress ultimately had sixteen children her motherly qualities were never in question!

October 1762 was a foundation stone for Mozart's fortunes in later life: with Maria Theresia's thirteen surviving children scattered in positions of power throughout Europe, imperial patronage of Mozart was to spread far and wide. Leopold especially was a fervent and devoted royalist, for whom the Imperial Family could do no wrong.

The magnificent Imperial Palace of Schönbrunn had been completely rebuilt in 1696 by Emperor Josef I after its devastation by the Turks thirteen years before. It was further renovated by Empress Maria Theresia twenty years before the Mozarts' arrival in Vienna. Very little has been altered since then, the most significant renovation being in 1945, as a result of bomb damage in the Second World War. Fortunately much of the priceless furniture and fittings were hidden away in the salt mines at the time.

Detail from "Serenade in Redoutensaal der Wiener Hofburg, Oktober 1760" by Meytens. Leopold and Wolfgang Mozart are positioned near the centre.

By courtesy of Kunsthistorisches Museum, Vienna.

The room where Wolferl and Nannerl entertained the Imperial Family is the gorgeously elegant Hall of Mirrors, in which the crystal mirrors built into the gilded wall panelling emphasize the white and gold baroque grandeur of the room.

The Hall of Ceremonies contains some interesting paintings, the most intriguing, from a Mozart point of view, being the 'Serenade in the Redoutensaal in The Hofburg, October 1760'. Near the bottom right hand corner of the picture stands a little boy of about six, with his father. The little boy is Wolfgang Amadeus Mozart, with his father Leopold. This anachronism is a mild case of artistic license, added at a later date, since the Mozarts certainly were not in Vienna at that time. However, it does show a degree of imperial recognition for a rare talent.

But where is Nannerl, one might ask oneself?

The Mozarts enjoyed the freedom of the palace, and Wolferl had no protocol qualms about running noisily around the corridors of Schönbrunn like a typical boisterous six year old. He readily made friends with everyone, including seven year old Princess Marie-Antoinette, who was later to become Queen of France. Legend has it that, while playing in the corridors of Schrönbrunn, Wolferl slipped and fell. All the other children laughed except for Marie-Antoinette, who helped him up, whereupon Wolferl said to her, 'You are kind; when I grow up I will marry you.'

The troth was plighted, but not, alas, fulfilled, for the little princess married Louis XVI instead, with consequences that led to the guillotine during the French Revolution.

But Wolferl was especially friendly with thirteen year old Princess Joanna, who took personal charge of him. She took him by the hand round the appartments of Schönbrunn, showed him her own rooms and generally looked after him.

Wherever they performed, the Mozarts were not only well paid, but were also provided with transport, both by the Imperial Family and by the noble houses. The Emperor sent 100 ducats to the Mozarts, and Leopold started thinking about buying his own carriage.

As for the Empress, she sent court clothes for the children. It was a source of great pride for the Mozarts,

Detail from the tomb of the Princess Joanna in the Habsburg Vaults in the Augustinerkirche, Vienna.

Source: Załuski photograph.

back home in Salzburg later the following year, when both children had their first portraits painted by Pietro Antonio Lorenzoni in clothes given by the Empress. In these portraits Wolferl wore the same lilac and gold costume which had originally been made for the little Archduke Maximilian; and Nannerl wore a pretty pink court dress which was also a present from the Empress.

Leopold himself enjoyed imperial patronage in his own right. His thesis on violin-playing, the *Violinschule*, was a significant, possibly even definitive publication much respected by players and teachers alike. He was a very fine violinist, and Wolfgang's skill on the instrument testified to his father's prowess as a teacher as well as a performer.

The Emperor's eldest son, the Archduke Joseph – later to become Emperor Joseph II – had recently married the Infanta Isabella of Parma, a granddaughter of King Louis XV of France. The young couple were ideally suited and very much in love, and graced the court of Vienna with their charm and good looks. The Infanta also played the violin, and the Emperor asked Leopold to listen to her playing and to give advice. Leopold readily complied with the imperial wish, and spent some time with the Infanta – although his opinion of her playing is not documented.

It was, therefore, a sad occasion for Leopold the following year when he heard that the Infanta had died of smallpox, leaving her young widower devastated. The Mozarts were in Paris at the time, and the period of mourning affected the Parisian court – and the Mozarts' fortunes.

About two weeks after their arrival, the Mozarts moved to lodgings in Fierberggassl, where they lived in somewhat cramped conditions. Leopold wrote that it was:

> 'close to the Hohe Bridge, in the house of the cabinet maker, on the first floor. The room is a thousand steps long and one step wide. You laugh? – to us it is not at all funny when we tread on each other's corns. Still less is it funny when my boy throws me, and the girl throws my wife, out of bed, or when they kick us in the ribs as they do every night. Each bed has a span of four and a half feet, and this amazing palace is divided by a

screen into two parts for each of these large beds. Patience! We are in Vienna.'

Today, the site is at Tiefer Graben 16, one block beyond the Collalto Palace in Am Hof. It was here that Wolferl became ill with spots and a fever. The symptoms included pain in the feet and hips and may well have been rheumatic fever. The spots spread and the fever continued unabated for a week, despite the application of Leopold's favourite remedy, *pulvis epilepticus niger* –his 'black powder', and he had to cancel all engagements.

October 31st, was Wolferl's name-day. He received greetings from the Hagenauers, and his father bought him a manuscript book. 'Wolfgangerl sends his obedient thanks for your good wishes for his name-day,' wrote Leopold to Lorenz Hagenauer. 'He wishes that he had had the good fortune not to have spent it in bed, although he felt better.'

And to cap it all, Wolferl was also suffering from toothache.

After a week Leopold met Countess von Sinzendorf's physician, Doctor Bernhard, who came to examine Wolferl and diagnosed a kind of scarlet fever rash. He then tended and looked after the little boy, and paid regular visits, and by the beginning of November Wolferl had largely recovered. 'Thank God it is now all right!' wrote Leopold on November 6th. 'Yesterday we repaid our good Doctor Bernhard with a concert. He invited many of his good friends to his house and sent his carriage for us.'

And so the round of concerts continued, but at a reduced rate, since the nobles, afraid of infection, were put off by Wolferl's lingering spots, and cashflow became a serious problem.

On the bright side, however, the Mozarts won five lottery prizes on five tickets!

On November 9th Wolferl played at a concert arranged by the Marquise Pacheco, at the house of Count Joseph Windischgraetz, near the Schwarzen Tor. Today, the site is at Bangasse 7.

By December, Leopold should have been, strictly speaking back in Salzburg, since he did not have unlimited leave from his duties as a second violinist and court composer at the Archbishop's court. Through a series of excuses, he managed to extend his stay in Vienna – some may say a foolhardy attitude for one seeking promotion to the post of vice kappellmeister. However, Leopold was banking on the fact that his family was gaining a very considerable reputation in the Austrian capital, thereby showering Salzburg with glory. The Archbishopric was considered somewhat backward, provincial and unsophisticated at the time, so the publicity gained could only be a good thing for the archbishop, who consequently desisted from making an issue out of it.

Also, Lorenz Hagenauer's daughters, Ursula and Francesca, had contracted smallpox, so Leopold was reluctant to return yet. 'It is as well that we are not at your house now!' wrote Leopold – somewhat tactlessly. 'We fear smallpox, and it might come up the stairs to us – now you know the reason why we do not want to come home.'

In December, Princess Joanna died of typhus at Schönbrunn. Wolferl had a particular affection for the young princess, who had been so kind and hospitable to him at the palace. He was especially upset by this event.

'Her Majesty the Empress has lost another princess,' wrote Leopold, 'namely Princess Joanna who was thirteen years old. She took my Wolferl by his hand when we were with her at court, and led him in and out of her rooms.'

In the meantime, due largely to the machinations of Count Palffy, there were invitations to the Mozarts from the nobles of Pressburg, at that time an important Hungarian city in the Empire, which today is the Czechoslovak city of Bratislava. So on December 11th the family set off by boat, and reached Pressburg, which was situated on the northern bank of the Danube, later that day.

The Mozarts stayed in Pressburg for nearly a fortnight, and gave several concerts, none of which is documented, except that they were well paid. Consequently, Leopold was able to afford to buy a well-sprung, closed, four-seater coach.

They had intended to return to Vienna on the 20th, spend Christmas there, and set off back to Salzburg on December 26th in order to be home by New Year's Eve. But they were delayed by the bitter cold weather which had made travelling conditions difficult, as, according to Leopold, 'the Hungarians do not build roads.' Besides, the post road ran along the south bank of the Danube, and a pontoon bridge, consisting of many rafts lashed together, was at that time the only way across. This pontoon bridge had been removed, and no carriage could get over.

To cap it all, it was Leopold's turn to have severe toothache!

The only way back to Vienna meant a winding, tortuous, cross-country route on the north side of the Danube. Besides being a long way round, it was also pockmarked with holes, ruts and ridges which made for a very uncomfortable ride, especially in frozen conditions. It also had the added disadvantage of being bisected by the River Morava, or March, a tributary which joined the Danube from the north, several kilometres upstream. Being a much smaller river than the Danube, it sometimes froze over, as it did on this occasion, although the Mozarts had to wait a couple of days for this to happen so that their carriage could get across safely.

Bratislava, the capital of Slovakia, is about seventy kilometres from Vienna. The city is dominated by the imposing, 10th century Bratislava Castle, standing sentinel over the Danube. Concerts are held in the Hall of the Slovak Philharmonic, as well as in the eighteenth century Primate's Palace, and in the Castle itself.

Today the post road is route 9, which connects Vienna and Bratislava along the south side of the Danube.

At half past eight on the morning of Christmas Eve, the Mozarts set off from Pressburg on their bumpy ride back to Vienna, where they arrived, cold and exhausted, at half past eight in the evening.

'Had I not bought a coach in Pressburg which is really well-hung, we would all have arrived with broken ribs.'

On their return, Leopold found that Countess Kynstky, at whose residence the Mozarts had already played on October 14th, 'had inquired every day whether we were back. On Christmas Day I went to see her and she said that she had waited for us anxiously, and had postponed a dinner for Field Marshal Daun, because he wanted to meet us. She gave this dinner on Monday.'

Leopold's planned departure for home, therefore, was further delayed in order to accommodate the Countess' invitation for December 27th, and the Mozarts finally set off back home to Salzburg on New Year's Eve in their new carriage. All that is known of the return trip was that they called at Linz and reached home on January 5th 1763, having taken the post route, which today is route 1 all the way. It leads out of Vienna, past Schönbrunn, through the rolling woodlands of the Wienerwald, and onto the broad, Danube plain all the way to Salzburg.

Although there is no evidence, the Mozarts may well have stopped at Melk and Ybbs, and it is more than likely that they stayed once more in Linz with the warm-hearted Kiener sisters. After Linz, they left the Danube and tackled the final leg back to Salzburg by way of Lambach.

Lambach boasts a Benedictine monastery where, in 1767, Mozart lunched and played the organ. He also took his wife Constanza there in 1783.

'I strolled into the church where a service was going on,' wrote Vincent Novello. 'It is a remarkably handsome one in the interior and is decorated with some very good paintings especially the large ones on the left side as you go up the nave.'

The church is now renowned mainly for its Romanesque frescoes, found in what was the choir of the original church, before it was rebuilt in the middle of the seventeenth century. After they were uncovered, they were lovingly restored in the 1960s, and can be viewed today on guided tours.

The abbey's organ, built in 1657 by Christoph Egedacher of Straubing, in Bavaria, is the original instrument that Mozart played on in 1767, and 1783.

It is possible that they may have stopped at Vöcklabruck, although it is unlikely that they would have lingered. It was bitterly cold, and no doubt Leopold could hardly wait to get home and recount his family's success story over coffee at his favourite haunt, Tomaselli's Cafe in the Alter Markt, which is still there.

Wolferl, on the other hand, promptly developed a severe attack of rheumatic fever as soon as the family arrived home. Unlike his father, he had to wait until he was better before he could tell everyone all about how he played the clavier for the Emperor, and sat on the Empress' knee and kissed her!

THE GRAND TOUR

Prelude

Controversy persists to this day as to whether Leopold Mozart was justified in dragging his two young children round the courts of Europe for months, even years, at a time. Is a rare talent in a very young child something that proud parents should promote for the sake of their children and the world at large, or does it constitute callous exploitation? Does extensive travel enrich a young child's mind, or does it deprive him or her of the stability of a normal home life? Reading between the lines of the Mozart story offers insights into both points of view.

There is no doubt that Wolferl Mozart was a singularly gifted child, his sister Nannerl a very talented girl, and Leopold an ambitious parent.

If omens are anything to go by, then the grand tour planned by Leopold during the early stages of 1763 certainly got off to a disastrous start when, just two hours short of their first post halt, one of the back wheels of their coach broke.

The Mozarts had only been on the road for a matter of hours when it happened. Everyone alighted from the stricken coach, and surveyed the broken wheel with dismay.

First there was Leopold Mozart, wishing now that he had listened to the advice of his friends back in Salzburg, who had all warned him that the coach was none too strong, and would never survive the rigours of an extended European tour. But Leopold, ever the optimist, had chosen to disregard the advice. Anyway, he was very proud of his coach, which he had bought only the previous winter in Pressburg (now Bratislava) on the proceeds of the family's first trip to Vienna.

Although he was undoubtedly a man of culture and sophistication, Leopold was not above uttering a curse under his breath to Sebastian Winter; and if documentation is anything to go by, then one can safely speculate that the language would certainly have been lacking in all culture and sophistication.

Sebastian Winter was Leopold's servant – specifically his valet/hairdresser. Leopold considered that if one were to travel around the courts of Europe, one would have to make a good impression and travel in style; and he considered a servant – as well as a private carriage – to be an essential appendage to his entourage.

Beside him stood his wife Maria Anna. Not a woman of any significant musical or intellectual standing, she was nonetheless a caring, fussing mother and a devoted, loving wife whose only concern was the well-being of her gifted family. Next there were Nannerl, now aged twelve, and her brother Wolferl now aged seven. Hovering in the background was the hired driver, whose curses were probably more audible than Leopold's as he saw his chances of an early stop to eat and to rest the horses for the night vanish.

It was a fine June evening, so Leopold and Sebastian Winter set off into the Bavarian countryside in search of help. At a mill a miller agreed to sell them a spare wheel. With much relief, Leopold and his servant returned to the coach and set about replacing the broken wheel, only to find that the new wheel was too small.

Although it was just about possible to get the coach going it swerved about dangerously, and the driver was barely able to control the horses.

In the end, Sebastian suggested, 'hewing down a small tree to bind in the front of the wheel, so that it should not run away.'

Having thus improvised, they lashed the iron parts of the broken wheel to the undercarriage, and set off gingerly into the gathering dusk. 'Sebastian and I,' wrote Leopold to Lorenz Hagenauer, 'travelled the rest of the way on foot so that our heavy bodies caused the wounded carriage no fresh hardship.'

It was past midnight when the wounded carriage finally

limped into Wasserburg, where they put up, sore and exhausted, at Zum Goldenen Stern.

Leopold Mozart had been employed as assistant kappellmeister at the court of the Archbishop of Salzburg, Count Sigismund von Schrattenbach for a year. His salary was not large, but he did enjoy one very important perk; the Archbishop was willing to allow him time off to travel with his children. After all, the Mozarts had returned from Vienna in January 1763 with a prestigious imperial seal of approval, which certainly deserved some recognition. Leopold, flushed with the success of the Vienna trip, immediately started making plans for a Grand Tour, with the conquest of a whole range of grand courts in mind.

The Archbishop, ever mindful of further prestige, was quite happy to grant Leopold leave of absence to travel; it was common practice in the eighteenth century for court musicians to visit other countries, if only to spy on other courts, tap their resources, or to gain experience.

And so, on a fine morning on June 9th, 1763, the Grand Tour began outside the Mozarts' Salzburg home in the Getreidegasse. A driver and horses had been hired to take them along the attractive post road to Wasserburg, which cut through thick forests, lakes and rolling Bavarian farmlands.

Today, the post road starts as the Ignaz Harrer Strasse, which leads out of Salzburg to the north-west, towards the German border town of Freilassing. From here the road goes past Waging, Traunreut and Stein. Just before Stein the road meets the 304 towards Munich, by way of Wasserburg.

Wasserburg-am-Inn is a beautifully placed, picturesque Bavarian town, situated on an amphitheatre of hills surrounding the River Inn. The post house, Zum Goldenen Stern is no longer there, but in its place stands a pharmacy, aptly named Apotheke-Stern, after the 'star' in the inn's name. A plaque commemorating the Mozart connection is to be found on the wall.

No sooner had the Mozarts booked in at Zum Goldenen Stern on that fateful first night, than a cartwright and a smith were summoned forthwith to deal with the problem of the broken wheel. It took two days to fix the wheel, and the Mozarts were forced to spend three nights in Wasserburg, much to Leopold's chagrin, before the wheel was finally repaired.

'The cartwright chopped and sawed, the smith singed and burned and hammered hard,' recorded Leopold as he anxiously watched his wheel being repaired.

The rest of the time was spent in looking round the town, and visiting the church of St Jacob (which is still there in the Kirchplatz), where Wolferl tried his hand – and his feet – at the organ. Leopold considered that trying out organs throughout Europe was an integral part of Wolferl's musical education. The policy paid off, for, in later life, Mozart considered the organ as being the king of instruments.

'We visited the organ during our stay and I explained the way to use the pedal to Wolferl,' wrote Leopold, 'and at once he tried it, pushing away the stool and standing on the pedal, as if he had practised it for many months. Everyone was amazed!'

By Sunday morning, June 12th, the coach was fully repaired, and the family set off for Munich.

ACT

1

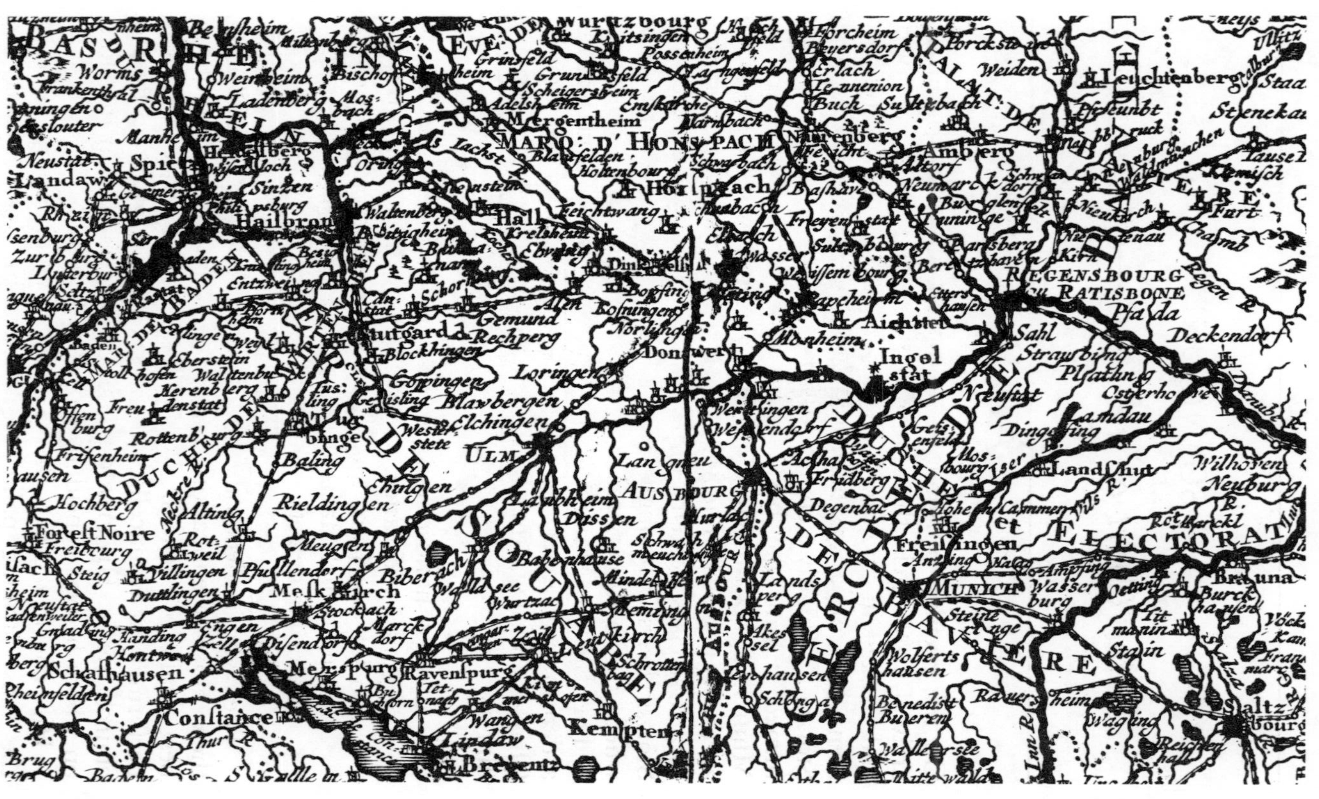

REGENSBOURG
RATISBONE
MUNICH
ULM
AUSBOURG
Constance
Kempten
Ingol stat
Hailbron
Stutgard
Nurenberg
Amberg
Leuchtenberg
Mergentheim
Schafhausen
Landshut
Freisingen
Deckendorf

SCENE ONE

At the Court of the Elector of Bavaria

On the evening of Sunday, June 12th, the Mozarts finally arrived in Munich, the seat of the Bavarian Electoral court, and booked in at Zum Goldenen Hirschen. This establishment became a gasthof in 1728, when Joseph Heinrich Störzer, a highly reputable wine retailer, bought it and turned it into the best – and most expensive – inn in Munich. It became familiarly known simply as 'Störzers', an accolade in itself. The inn flourished in the Störzer family as a first class hostelry until 1823, when it was sold by the Störzer heirs. Although the inn no longer exists, its site is where 18 Theatinerstrasse stands today.

The Elector Maximilian III Joseph of Bavaria was an ardent music lover, as indeed were his predecessors. Dr Charles Burney, the English musical traveller, describes him as:

> 'a very handsome and gracious prince, has an elegant appearance, and a figure, which is neither too fat, too lean, too tall, nor too short, if I were not too much dazzled by his condescension, to see any of his defects.'

The whole electoral family were talented performers, their musical education having been in the hands of the best Italian teachers. Maximilian Joseph was no mean performer on violincello, and also composed a good deal of church music. His greatest talent, however, lay in the flute, on which he was considered to be a virtuoso.

His court was at the Schloss Nymphenburg, one of the most striking palace complexes in Germany. It was originally built between 1664–74, with more buildings added during ensuing decades, specifically the Pagodenburg overlooking the smaller of the two ornamental lakes, the Kleiner See; the Badenburg, or Bathhouse, standing sentinel over the larger Grosser See; the Magdalenenklause, and, the most splendid of them all, if only for the Hall of Mirrors, the Amalienburg, designed by F. Cuvilliés the Elder and built by Elector Carl Albrecht.

Leopold Mozart saw no reason to waste time in idle tourism, and first thing on the morning of Monday, June 13th, he bundled his family into the coach and drove straight to the Nymphenburg Palace. They parked the coach outside, and went into the grounds of the palace in search of the Elector.

By chance they were seen through a window by Prince Friedrich Michael von Zweibrücken, whom Leopold had met previously in Vienna.

The House of Zweibrücken were the heirs to the Palatine court in Mannheim, and featured in the Mozart story on several occasions. The Prince recognized the Mozart family as they walked up and down the grounds and terraces looking for someone who might point them in the right direction.

The Prince, surprised and delighted at the prospect of meeting the Mozarts again, beckoned to them from the window, and enquired whether the Elector was expecting them. Leopold replied that they were, in fact, looking for an audience with the Elector with a view to giving a performance at the court. The Prince immediately took the matter in hand, and sent a courtier to the Elector with a message that the Mozart family were in Munich, and were offering their services.

To Leopold's delight, the message came back that the Elector would be pleased to listen to them that very evening at the Palace.

To kill time before the concert was due to begin, Leopold took his family to see the grounds and buildings of the Palace. Unfortunately, the weather changed for the worse, for when they reached the Badenburg, they were caught in a downpour.

Wolferl duly performed at the concert that evening, and

was a great success. He played the clavier, extemporized, and played a concerto for violin and clavier with his father.

The Elector was most impressed, and Leopold hoped that a 'present' would be forthcoming in due course. 'Present' was a euphemism for payment, a word which, with its obviously financial connotation, was considered vulgar. Leopold was anxious about the size of the present since Herr Störzer's bill would be devoid of all such niceties.

The family arrived back at Störzers at a quarter past eleven, when they had supper and went to bed very late, long past a seven year old's bedtime.

Wolferl must have been exhausted after such a busy day, although he may well have been far too excited at first to sleep, having performed at such a magnificent court, in front of such splendid musicians, and making his father very proud of him! As for Leopold, no doubt he quietly congratulated himself on a job well done, and day well spent.

The following two evenings, Wolfgang played for Duke Clemens, the Elector's brother, who was also extremely impressed with their performance, and positively eulogized about little Wolfgang. He wrote the Mozarts a letter of recommendation to the Elector Karl Theodor of the Palatinate, at his court in Mannheim, as well as one to the Electress.

Leopold noted ruefully that on these two occasions, no 'presents' were forthcoming, and the price of Herr Störzer's hospitality began to loom larger than ever.

However, Wolferl's success was considerable, and Prince Friedrich von Zweibrücken, who happened to be departing for the Palatinate, promised to inform that Elector of the impending arrival of the Mozart family in his city of Mannheim.

By June 21st, the day before the Mozarts' departure, Leopold was extremely worried. 'What our bill at the end will be,' he wrote apprehensively, 'we shall have the honour to hear tomorrow. Herr Störzer has a reputation not only for good service, but also for writing bills.'

Fortunately, the Elector Maximilian Joseph summoned Nannerl to play for him that day. She had not been asked to perform on the Mozarts' first visit to the Nymphenburg

Palace, and now the Elector had expressed a wish to hear her after all.

He was 'gracious' enough to give Leopold a 'present' of 100 gulden. Shortly afterwards, a further 75 gulden arrived from Duke Clemens. Etiquette forbade him from exceeding his brother's payment, so he had no option but to wait and see what the Elector's payment would be before he could arrive at a relatively correct figure.

On the morning of June 22nd, a much relieved Leopold was well able to pay the good Herr Störzer his dues, and bade the newly hired driver to set off for Augsburg.

SCENE TWO

At the Court of the King of Rücken

Most little boys invent fantasy lands at some time during the course of their childhoods, and the more creative the child, the more complex is the fantasy land. Wolferl was no exception. Aided and abetted by the servant Sebastian Winter, he invented the land of Rücken, of which he was king. He ruled over his subjects firmly, fairly and with considerable creative flair. The Kingdom of Rücken differed from the realms of reality in one particular facet: everything was backwards. "Rück" itself is the German word for "back". Tradition has it that the "backwards" concept came to Wolferl as a result of sitting with his back to the horses in the coach, which gave the illusion of the world passing by backwards – although this is pure speculation, since backwards lands have always featured very prominently in children's fantasy lands.

In the same way that today's children relieve the boredom of endless journeys with games such as 'I-spy', Wolferl's escape was an endless tapestry of backwards situations and backwards writing to relieve the tedium and discomfort of long distance travel.

His kingdom came into its own during the long stretches of the Grand Tour, which must have felt to the Mozarts like a round the world trip would feel to us in our present century in sheer size and scope. The fact that Sebastian, no doubt still a boy at heart, joined in the fun, must have helped; and coupled with the sights and sounds of strange new lands with equally strange customs and languages, must have inspired the young composer to ever greater forays into fantasy.

In later years, the adult Nannerl made several references

to her younger brother's magic land, and even mentioned that Wolferl and Sebastian used to make maps of Rücken as well. Rücken stayed with Wolfgang well into adulthood, and he had been known to write his name 'Trazom' on a number of future occasions, either as a pseudonym, or as a joke.

An interesting variant on the 'I-spy' principle would be post house spotting, an historical game as much for adults as for children. Travelling along old post routes, one can hardly fail to come across the original post inns; most have changed completely; some are nineteenth century buildings, built when new post routes opened up, and some have grown into first class, modern hotels. There are a number which still stand as they did in the eighteenth century, having been lovingly cared for and preserved in their original state. Post inns are easily recognizable, not only because they call themselves 'post hotel', but also by their posthorn motif, or a wrought iron coach-and-horses sign. The Mozarts would have stopped at quite a few of them, if only for a meal, a coffee, or to change horses.

Augsburg, Leopold's birthplace, is about seventy kilometres from Munich along what today is route 2, a day's journey by coach. The city suffered severe bombing on February 25th 1944, and many of the Mozart sites were destroyed. However the house where Leopold Mozart was born, at 30 Frauentorstrasse, survived, and is now a Mozart memorial and museum, even though it is more Leopold than Wolfgang oriented. This is the premier Mozart site in Augsburg, and it contains much information about the Mozart family, their roots and their history.

On the evening of June 22nd, the Mozarts booked in at the Drei Mohren inn, in Maximilianstrasse. The hotel is still there, although it has been rebuilt several times and considerably enlarged. It is now the Steigenberger Drei Mohren Hotel.

'Herr Linay, who is the most agreeable man in the world,' wrote Leopold about the proprietor, 'kept me very well.'

Later, however, he did add that it was 'uncommonly dear and our takings had to be spent. It cost 95 florins for the 16 day stay.'

The takings in question were the proceeds of three

Hotel of the 3 Moors at Augsburg

J. G. Deuringers Gasthof
zu den Drey Mohren
Maximilians-Strasse in Augsburg.
vormals der Pallast Anton Fuggers des Reichen;
wurde von Kaiser Carl den Fünften, Anno 1530
während des berühmten Reichstags bewohnt.

The "Drei Mohren" hotel in Augsburg, in eighteenth century and today.

By courtesy of Drei Mohren Hotel.

concerts given by the children in Augsburg, on June 28th and 30th, and July 4th. They were given at the inn, Zu den Drei Königen, which was destroyed in 1944. The site is at Jakoberstrasse 28. Leopold complained bitterly that the audience were all Lutherans, and that the Catholics stayed away. Being a staunchly Catholic family, the Mozarts were very disappointed that their fellow adherents did not appreciate them, especially since their roots were in that city.

But then, Augsburg suffered considerably from religious bigotry on which local politics were based. What was embraced by one faction tended to be eschewed by the other as a matter of principle.

The family visited Leopold's brother, Franz Alois Mozart, in Jesuitengasse, very close to the Cathedral. The house itself is no longer there, and its exact site is not known.

Not so the Fuggerei, built between 1516 and 1523, which is the world's oldest welfare housing estate. Mozart's great grandfather Franz lived here, at No 10, from 1681 to 1693. A plaque on the wall commemorates this fact.

Leopold took Wolferl and Nannerl round to see the sights of Augsburg. He showed them the famous Goldener Saal on the first floor in the Rathaus. Although badly damaged in 1944, the Rathaus has been restored to its former grandeur, and the superb hall, in which Wolfgang almost certainly played in 1790, is one of Augsburg's finest examples of German Baroque. They also saw the treasures in the fine baroque church of St Ulrich, on whose organ Wolferl played in 1777.

During the course of his stay, Leopold met many people, especially members of the Collegium Musicum, of whom the most significant was the organ and clavier builder, Johann Andreas Stein (1728–92). He showed the Mozarts his handiwork, including the organ in the Barfüsser church, which no longer exists. Stein's craftsmanship was of a high standard, and his reputation grew steadily both in Germany and abroad. He counted both Mozart and Beethoven as devotees of his work. Mozart, in later years, considered his claviers to be the best.

Leopold even purchased from Stein 'a pretty little clavier,

which will be of great service to us for practising during our travels.' It became one of the Mozarts' most treasured possessions.

A strong friendship was forged between the Mozarts and Stein, and Wolfgang called on him again in later years, both personally and professionally.

One incident in Augsburg may serve as a significant pointer in the for/against debate with regard to children being taken on long, performing tours. Wolferl woke up one morning and began to cry. When asked what was the matter, he sobbed that he was missing his friends from Salzburg: Wenzl, Spitzeder, Deibl, Leutgeb, Vögt, as well as Lorenz, Cajetan and Nazerl Hagenauer . . .

All in all, the Mozarts' fortnight in Augsburg yielded little by way of fame and fortune, although expenses were covered, and the Mozarts came away with many new friends and acquaintances, not to mention their new clavier.

On the morning of July 6th, it was a disappointed Leopold who hired fresh horses and a new driver, and bade him to make for Ulm, their next port of call, about 100 kilometres to the west, along what is today route 10. They arrived in Ulm that same night, and booked into Zum Goldenes Rad in the shadow of Ulm Cathedral. The Goldenes Rad is now a first class, modern hotel.

SCENE THREE

The Parade of the Tin Soldiers

One of the people that Leopold met in Augsburg was Pietro Nardini (1722–93), a virtuoso violinist from Tuscany, and a pupil of Tartini (1692–1770). Leopold was singularly impressed by the 'beauty, purity, evenness of tone and singing quality' of his playing. Nardini, in turn, was enchanted by Leopold's talented children, and told him about his post as violinist at the court of Duke Karl Eugen of Württemberg, who had a first-class orchestra.

At this time, the best musical education in Europe was to be found in Italy, and Italian teachers were venerated and much sought after. One of the most influential figures in Italian musical spheres was the kappellmeister to the court of Duke Karl Eugen of Württemberg, Niccolo Jomelli (1714–74). He counted Christian Cannabich, who was to play such an important part in Mozart's fortunes, among his star pupils.

Nardini strongly recommended that the Mozarts should make a point of visiting Duke Karl Eugen at his court in Ludwigsburg, just a short distance from the official ducal seat at Stuttgart, and approaching Niccolo Jomelli about giving a performance.

Leopold decided to waste no time in getting to Ludwigsburg as quickly as possible, which is why they only spent one night in the lovely city of Ulm, situated on a still young River Danube.

The following morning, July 7th, there were no fresh horses to be found, so, having despatched Sebastian to find some, Leopold took advantage of the delay to take his children to see the fourteenth century Gothic Minster in the Münsterplatz, just beside the Goldenes Rad.

Today, Ulm Cathedral is one of the most magnificent and imposing churches in all Germany. The modern visitor is overawed by the sheer height of the main tower – at nearly 162 metres it is among the tallest in Europe, although in Mozart's day it was only 70 metres tall.

Wolferl, once more, played on the two-manual organ, under the supervision of both his father and Herr Walther, the organist. The original organ is no longer there; the two present organs were installed in the 1960s. The Mozarts also visited the Wengenkirche in Wengengasse, the older remains of which are now preserved within a modern building.

Eventually the family moved off, slightly behind schedule, passing through the old Swabian town of Geislingen situated where five valleys meet. The Novellos wrote of it: 'Geislingen in the mountains seems a most romantic place.'

The Mozarts proceeded on to Göppingen, and Plochingen, in the approaches to Stuttgart, where they stopped to change horses at Zum Ochsen. Here the postmaster warned Leopold that if he wanted to catch the Duke of Württemberg, he would have to hurry, since the Duke was arranging a hunt, and was preparing to depart for his hunting lodge in Grafeneck on the 10th. The inn is still there, now renamed Zum Waldhorn.

Since it was now the 8th, Leopold thanked the man and bade the driver spur the steeds, and made off towards Cannstatt, bypassing Stuttgart, and on to Ludwigsburg, where they booked in the following day at Zum Goldenen Waldhorn. The building is still there, opposite the entrance to the castle; today it is a Chinese restaurant, and bears a plaque to commemorate the Mozarts' visit.

The Castle is impressive with an enormous quadrangle, which served as the parade ground where Karl Eugen's soldiers used to be put through their paces.

Karl Eugen, the Duke of Württemberg, in common with most German aristocrats, had three overwhelming passions: the Military, Music and Hunting, all of which, in the case of Württemberg, accounted for more than their fair share of the state budget. Charles Burney points out that Ludwigsburg seemed to consist 'half of stage-players, fiddlers and soldiers, and the other half of beggars.'

Added to this was the fact that Karl Eugen had abandoned Stuttgart in favour of Ludwigsburg as his seat, thus plunging the inhabitants of his official ducal city to economic ruin and decay through his absence.

Contrasts between rich and poor were very much in evidence in the beautiful state of Württemberg, which embraces, among other areas of outstanding natural beauty, the Swabian National Park.

'From Geislingen to Ludwigsburg,' wrote Leopold in tourist mode, 'one sees nothing to the right and left all the time but water, woods, fields, meadows, gardens and vineyards, all mixed together in the loveliest way.'

Burney in 1772 wrote that 'the country . . . is very fertile, especially in vines, producing a great quantity of what is called Neckar wine.'

That other great musical traveller, Edward Holmes, went further, when he commented, in 1828, that 'the produce of the Neckar vineyards which is there [Stuttgart] placed on the dinner table in unstopped decanters, has a strong resemblance in colour, smell and taste to the gargle which physicians prescribe for a sore throat.'

As far as the Military was concerned, Karl Eugen founded a military academy called the Karlsschule. This accounted for the innumerable soldiers that filled Ludwigsburg to capacity. Visitors came away awed by the spectacle of such military might – not always to Karl Eugen's credit. Burney was certainly struck by what he saw there in 1772 – 'The soldiers seem disciplined into clockwork. I never saw such exactness in animated beings.'

Vincent Novello was very scathing: 'The only thing I disliked [about Ludwigsburg] was the quantity of soldiers, who seemed to be more numerous than the inhabitants. I have an invincible repugnance to these outward signs of the power of the privileged few . . .'

More bemused were Leopold's comments:

> 'In the streets one hears incessantly "HALT! QUICK MARCH! RIGHT – LEFT!" and sees nothing but arms, drums and war material . . . I thought the soldiers looked like people in some Comedy or opera . . . They are all exactly alike,

> and every day their hair is set in many curls combed back from their face and powdered snow-white, and their beards are greased coal-black.'

Burney may have been awed, Vincent Novello disgusted, Leopold bemused – but Wolfgang must have loved them, and spent a great deal of time looking at them as their parade ground was exactly opposite the inn. After all, most seven year old boys love a parade of tin soldiers!

As far as Music was concerned, Karl Eugen's orchestra had been favourably compared to that of Mannheim, whose excellence and style under the leadership of Stamitz and – later – Cannabich, set the standards by which all European orchestras came to be judged. With Niccolo Jomelli as kappellmeister, the Württemberg orchestra was filled with Italians, promoting the Italian style to the callous and unfair exclusion of all German talent.

At least, that is what Leopold maintained as he seethed with disgust when, having arrived in Ludwigsburg and showed off his childrens' prowess, Jomelli was most impressed, but regretted that the Duke would not be in a position to hear the Mozarts performing, since he was busy preparing for his departure the following day for Grafeneck, his hunting lodge fourteen hours distant from Ludwigsburg.

Leopold had misunderstood the third great German aristocratic passion – the Hunt. Huge expanses of Karl Eugen's realm were given over for this purpose. 'The expense is generally enormous,' writes Charles Burney. 'Immense forests and parks, set aside for a prince's amusement, at the expense of agriculture, commerce and indeed, the necessities of life, keep vast tracts of land uncultivated, and his subjects in beggary.'

True to style, all other activities were suspended when a hunt was imminent, and Leopold was surely being very optimistic if he counted on the Duke dropping his preparations to listen to a pair of children from provincial Salzburg!

Despite being blamed, Jomelli was very flattering – if not a little jingoistic! – about Wolfgang's playing, when he commented that 'it was astonishing and scarcely believable that a German child could have such musical genius and so much spirit and brilliance!'

Today the post road from Ulm to Stuttgart is route 10 all the way, although strictly speaking the old route passed through the village of Westerstette, which is off the main road, about half way from Ulm to Geislingen. It detours to the right before rejoining the main road.

Just before Stuttgart the Mozart trail runs cold among the suburbs and motorways, and the actual post route between the Stuttgart suburb of Cannstatt and Ludwigsburg is now lost and redeveloped.

The Mozarts spent three nights in Ludwigsburg with nothing to show for their visit, apart from having met the iniquitous Niccolo Jomelli. It turned out during the Mozarts' first Italian journey, that Jomelli was not so iniquitous after all, for he became a good friend to the Mozarts, and an important musical influence on Wolfgang. As indeed did Nardini, whom they also met that same year.

In the meantime, before he went to sleep each night, little Wolferl possibly thought about the 'twelve to fifteen thousand soldiers who strut around every day unbelievably dressed up, who can scarcely walk on account of their tight gaiters and breeches.'

Except that his soldiers strutted backwards!

SCENE FOUR

At the Court of the Elector of the Palatinate

On the morning of July 12th, the Mozarts once more set off for the Palatine Court of Mannheim, which at the time was at its summer residence at Schwetzingen. The road took them through Enzweihingen, 'altogether Lutheran, and a miserable spot,' according to Leopold, and on to Bruchsal, where they put up for the night at 'Zum Riesen'. This was obviously not so miserable a spot since Leopold saw fit to spend a couple of days there, showing the children the palace of the Prince Bishops of Schönborn. He commented that, 'the rooms are of the best of good taste: not many rooms, however very noble, indescribably charming and costly, and one could not see anything more agreeable.'

The palace is indeed an outstanding example of baroque, originally built between 1722 and 1760, so it was a brand new complex that the Mozarts viewed on that summer morning in July. It also contained one of the most noteworthy examples of baroque architecture in the famous Bruchsal Staircase, built originally by Balthasar Neumann.

At the time, the incumbent Archbishop was Franz Christoph von Hütten, and according to a traditional source, Wolfgang played the clavier at a concert at the palace at which the Archbishop was present.

On the night of July 13th, there was a violent thunderstorm which lasted nearly all night. The Mozarts slept through the whole thing – except for Leopold. He lay awake, tormented by the memory of a house in flames that he saw a few days beforehand in Cannstatt. It had been struck by lightning during a similar storm, and now he was worried that the inn, being built of timber, would suffer a similar fate.

"Zum Roten Haus" in Schwetzingen, from a photograph taken in 1912. The inn was destroyed in 1920.

By courtesy of Stadtachiv, Schwetzingen.

The following morning, it was a bleary eyed Leopold who followed his rested and refreshed family into the coach for the next stage of their journey.

Unfortunately, the Schloss, the guest house 'Zum Riesen', as well as most of the town and its records were destroyed in the Second World War. The Schloss has now been meticulously and painstakingly rebuilt to its former glory and contains the Louis XVI chamber music room that is the venue of the annual concerts of eighteenth century music, which take place every June.

The post road from Ludwigsburg to Bruchsal first went south to Stuttgart – now lost among suburban redevopments – before rejoining route 10 and passing through Enzweihingen and Vaihingen. At Illingen, the road changes to route 35 and passes through Bretten and on to Bruchsal. After Bruchsal, the road continues along route 35 as far as the crossroads with route 36, which leads north to Schwetzingen.

The Mozarts arrived in Schwetzingen that same evening, booked in at 'Zum Roten Haus', and stayed for just under a week. This inn continued to function until it was finally closed in 1921. The site is today at Dreikönigstrasse 6, beside which stands a Mozart memorial.

Leopold went to see Baron Eberstein, the Director of Music, with Duke Clemens' letters of recommendation to both the Elector and the Electress. The Baron, having also received a glowing verbal report from Prince Friedrich von Zweibrücken, took due note, and the Mozarts gained instant admission to the Electoral concert hall.

July 18th was a beautiful day, and the Mozart children captivated the Palatine court at their summer residence at the Schloss with an evening of their own particular mixture of virtuosity and extemporization. Leopold and Nannerl both took part as well as Wolfgang, who played not only the clavier, but also the bells and glasses! Their success was resounding – in more ways than one!

'Yesterday a concert was held for us, one of only two since the end of May,' wrote Leopold excitedly. 'It lasted from 5 o'clock to 9 o'clock at night. My children,' he added in proud paternal mode, 'have excited all Schwetzingen and the Elector has shown indescribable pleasure and everyone is amazed!'

At this concert, the Mozarts met the eminent flautist of international repute, Johann Wendling (1723–97). Wolferl was to meet him again in later years, and forge a deep friendship and professional association with him. Leopold met the violinist in the orchestra, Johann Danner, whose five year old son, Christian, was following in his father's footsteps, and learning to play the violin. Christian Danner also became in later years a very close friend of Wolfgang.

The following day the Mozarts went, as guests, to attend a performance at the Rococo Theatre, which is situated in a wing of the Palace. The play, Nannerl noted in her travel diary, was a French comedy.

In the middle of the eighteenth century, the Mannheim-Schwetzingen circuit was undoubtedly the home of the finest, most revolutionary orchestra in Europe. Under the auspices of the music-loving Elector Karl Theodor, the Mannheim school was originally established by Johann Stamitz (1717–57) when he was appointed to the court orchestra in 1742. Stamitz took great pains with his orchestra, and directed it with far-seeing flair and inspiration. He introduced the concepts of dynamics, light and shade, good tone and orchestral colour. To achieve this, he also expected excellence of technical playing from his musicians, and exhorted them to practise a great deal, which is why contemporary chronicles speak of both Mannheim and Schwetzingen as being full of the sounds of music wherever one went.

Stamitz overturned the previously accepted norm of merely giving an orchestra the copied parts, which were instantly played without reference to dynamics or interpretation of any kind, often without rehearsal.

The Mannheim school fostered the growing popularity of the clarinet, as well as being responsible for the development of the classical Symphony and the Concerto. Stamitz himself wrote no less than seventy-four symphonies.

He also developed the principle of interpretation, in which his personality and musicianship came through in the music. He was undoubtedly the originator of the position of conductor as we understand the term today. Although he died in 1758, his legacy continued unabated.

The Elector spared no expense to ensure that his famous orchestra should continue to flourish. The numerous concerts were freely open not only to the resident population, but also to visitors, thus ensuring that the orchestra's reputation spread throughout Europe.

'To anyone walking through the streets of Schwetzingen during summer,' wrote Charles Burney, 'this place must seem to be inhabited only by a colony of musicians, who are constantly exercising their profession: at one house a fine player on the violin is heard; at another, a German flute; here an excellent oboe; there a bassoon, a clarionet, a violincello, or a concert of several instruments together.'

Leopold was also impressed by what he had heard – and seen: 'The orchestra is without doubt the best in Germany, with only young people of good character in it, who are neither drunkards, gamblers or loose-living, therefore both their conduct and their playing are to be admired.'

Two days after the concert, the Mozarts bade Schwetzingen a fond farewell, left 'Zum Roten Haus' and drove the short distance to Heidelberg, where Leopold particularly wanted to see the Schloss and the legendary Great Tun.

SCENE FIVE

The Great Tun

The Elector Karl Theodor's Palatinate of the Rhine was a very complex and uneasy melting pot of religions, as indeed was the whole of the Rhineland region. Leopold wrote of four religions somehow co-existing side by side: Catholic, Lutheran, Calvinist and Jewish. He had seen evidence of religious intolerance in Augsburg, and there was certainly an underlying current of unrest in Karl Theodor's realm. Leopold was a fervent Catholic, and his letters do more than hint at intolerance of other religions. He noted, for instance, the absence of crucifixes and holy water stoups. These were small, semi-circular bowls attached to the walls by the doors of rooms, similar to the ornate little fonts found in the entrances to churches and cathedrals, containing small quantities of water blessed by a priest. Devout Catholics used these stoups of holy water to dip their fingers in before crossing themselves as they entered a room.

Accustomed to such outward manifestations of his Faith, Leopold nonetheless reluctantly acknowledged that landlords had to dispense with all religious trappings lest they offend any guests.

Leopold, if not actually offended, was perhaps a little put out at not finding any of the familiar trappings that he had taken for granted all his life. Many of his later comments on religious observance throughout the region shed considerable light on his own prejudices.

> 'Certainly I must say that I am astonished at the dirtiness, negligence and right boorish style with which the church ceremonies in Mainz and Koblenz were received. It is no wonder when these

> parts are filled with Lutherans, Calvinists and Jews.'

He was further appalled at the lack of reverence shown during a funeral in St Peter's church in Mainz, where, 'everybody was chattering and talking, and in the middle stood the bier, it was an assembly of mourners for a dead official. And that is how they behave in these parts . . . Our court,' he added, referring to his hometown, 'is actually a doubly Roman Court and our gracious Archbishop is another Pope!'

The greatest prejudices existed between the three Christian sects, and the Jews, though generally despised, were left to their own devices. In 1765, Thomas Pennant wrote of the Jews of Frankfurt that:

> 'there are about 10,000 of that sect. They live in a particular quarter of the city. None are rich, and all lie under a bad character. They have the free exercise of their religion, as have the Catholics, which is more extraordinary as the Calvinists are obliged to go out of town for divine service; the government here is entirely Lutheran.'

Leopold also complained about the food, both from a religious as well as a gastronomic point of view. 'Fast dishes [as in frugal fare, or fish, specifically prepared for days of fasting and abstinence] are very difficult to buy, they prepare them badly because everyone eats meat, and who knows what they have served to us?'

Evidence of unbridled bigotry and hatred was certainly to be seen at the old seat of the Palatine court in Heidelberg, as the Mozarts soon discovered after they had booked in at Zu den drei Königen.

Surrounded by richly wooded hills, the University city of Heidelberg nestles athwart the banks of the River Neckar just before it enters the Rhine valley and merges with that great river at Mannheim, a situation that Leopold found very similar to that of Salzburg.

The best view of the city, as the Novellos found, is from the Philosophenweg, or Philosophers' way. This is a long, wide promenade, half way up the mountain on the north side, running parallel to the river. It commands a spectacular vista – one can see why it is so aptly named. It can be reached by a steep, winding footpath which starts at the north end of Alte Brücke, or the Karl Theodor Bridge. The Elector's statue stands on this bridge, next to the South Gate.

From the Philosophenweg can be seen the two large churches that are connected with the Mozarts' visit. The first is the imposing sixteenth century Church of the Holy Ghost, which Leopold took his family to see. From the Philosophenweg it can be seen just behind the baroque turrets of the South Gate of the Old Bridge.

'In the Church of the Holy Ghost, which is known in history on account of the struggle between the Catholics and the Calvinists,' wrote Leopold, 'our Wolfgang played the organ with such magic that in everlasting memory the Town Magistrate ordered that his name be inscribed with full particulars on the casing.'

The Church of the Holy Ghost, founded in 1400, is the biggest Gothic church in the Palatinate. It had been the focal point of a series of religious controversies, whereby it had been alternately Catholic and Lutheran, depending on the religious affiliation of the Elector at the time. It has even been partitioned to accommodate both factions, and it was not until 1936 that the partitions were finally taken down; the church is now Protestant.

Looking over the city from the Philosophenweg, a little to the right and further away, one sees the Jesuit Church. The organ at the Church of the Holy Ghost, on which Mozart played was removed to the Jesuit Church in 1808, but has since been replaced with a modern instrument. The original no longer exists; although tradition has it that part of the organ was bricked in, and might still be there. But there is no proof of this, so until the organ is again replaced the tradition must remain apocryphal.

Over to the left, dominating the whole city with its imposing presence, stands the Schloss. The Novellos described it as 'one of the most extensive and picturesque ruins,' as they themselves surveyed it from the Philosophenweg.

A view of Heidelberg and the Church of the Holy Ghost.

Source: Załuski photo.

The original Schloss dates back to the fourteenth century, and has had a very rich and turbulent history. For a long time it was the seat of the Palatine Court, and it was totally destroyed during the course of the Thirty Years War and the vicious French Wars that followed.

The Elector Karl Philipp, sickened by the religious intolerance, removed his court from Heidelberg to Mannheim in 1720, and the Schloss was left to crumble, and the city to decay.

The enlightened Elector Karl Theodor turned his attention to rebuilding his shattered Electorate, both physically and culturally. Not only did he found his Orchestra and Theatre in Mannheim, he also began an ambitious programme of reconstruction. He built the Schloss at Schwetzingen as a summer residence, and went on to tackle the ruins of the Schloss at Heidelberg. The rebuilding programme ran into considerable difficulties when lightning caused huge damage to completed buildings in 1764, a year after the Mozarts' visit, and all further work was suspended.

'And the fallen-in doors and walls in the Schloss which are quite remarkable,' wrote Leopold, 'show the sad fruits of the French wars.'

During their visit the Mozarts would have seen the Great Tun. This is an enormous barrel, housed in the Schloss, and finished in 1751 by Karl Theodor, which holds 221,726 litres of wine. Doubtless it was built to contain not only the fruits of the countless vineyards that lined the Neckar, but also all those spread out over the Rhineland Pfalz beyond the Rhine. All the Schloss cellars and vats together had a capacity of over 700,000 litres, and the average wine consumption at the time was 2,000 litres a day!

On the mountaintop directly above the Schloss, clearly visible from the Philosophenweg, is the Königstuhl, on which stands the Observatory. It contains the Visitors' Book from the Mannheim Observatory, which Mozart visited in 1778, and which he signed.

After Heidelberg, Leopold decided to spend three days at the hotel Zum Prinz Friedrich in Mannheim, only about ten kilometres away. Although the court was actually in Schwetzingen at the time, Leopold nevertheless decided to visit the official Electoral seat before moving on towards fresh, unknown pastures beyond the Rhine. In Mannheim the Mozarts gave a small concert to an unnamed French general, who presented a little ring to Nannerl, and a pretty toothpick case to Wolfgang.

Mannheim is a nuclear city laid out in the shape of a horseshoe. At the open end stands the Schloss and its gardens giving onto the Rhine, and the rounded end touches the banks of the Neckar.

The city is a masterpiece of planning, with straight roads criss-crossing each other to make up 144 grids, each one numbered and lettered as a grid reference.

A well-known department store in Mannheim grid reference F1 today marks the site of the Pfalzicher Hof, where Mozart stayed in 1777. The Jesuitenkirche, damaged in World War 2, stands in its original place, as does the Schloss, which today is a complex which houses, among other institutions, the University. The great hall and the court Kappelle, or chapel, scenes of significant music making and many visits by Mozart in later years, have also been rebuilt.

Leopold was very impressed with Mannheim.

> 'The town of Manheim is very beautiful because of its regularity," he wrote, 'but, because all the houses are only one storey high, it looks like a town in miniature. At the end of each street four streets meet in a cross, each street is exactly the same and each side is the same also. On each side of the street there is a gutter for the rainwater and there are painted sticks with lanterns which light up the dark night. You cannot imagine what a beautiful perspective this is when the streets are thus illuminated, as for example from the Castle to the Neckar Gate.'

Nannerl, in her childishly simple travel notes, mentions visits to the Palace, the Opera House, the Picture Gallery, the Library and the Treasure Chamber.

Finally on August 1st, the Mozarts, fifteen louis d'or the richer, left the heady atmosphere of the Palatinate's golden triangle of Mannheim-Schwetzingen-Heidelberg. They passed through Wörms, where they spent one night at Zum Schwan and dined with a Baron von Dalberg, before continuing northwards through Oppenheim to Mainz. 'If you want to see a bad road,' wrote Leopold to Lorenz Hagenauer, 'try the one from Wörms to Oppenheim.' He added that Oppenheim lay in ruins as a result of the French wars. After Oppenheim, when the road rejoined the Rhine, it improved. 'From Oppenheim to Mainz, it is extremely agreeable, with the Rhine close on one side, and on the left fields, villages, gardens and vineyards.'

They reached Mainz on the evening of August 3rd, and booked in at Zum König von England.

SCENE SIX

Wolferl's Rhine Journey

The River Rhine rises at two sources in the south eastern reaches of the Swiss Alps before uniting in Chur. Continuing its northward journey, it forms the frontier between Switzerland and the tiny Principality of Liechtenstein, then the frontier between Switzerland and Austria, before flowing into Lake Constance. From there it re-emerges to form the frontier between Switzerland and Germany, apart from a hiccup in the environs of Schaffhausen. At Basle it turns northwards, and forms the frontier between France and Germany, at least as far as the vicinity of Karlsruhe.

The Rhine is historically, commercially and spiritually the most important river in Germany.

The Mozarts covered a considerable length of its 1,200 kilometres that year.

The imaginative traveller may well contemplate its timeless flow and feel the full spectrum of the German experience: the mythology that produced the Rhine-maidens, along with the pollution that is the price, paid in Rhinegold, of a thriving modern state.

Along its course, the Rhine collects a number of secondary rivers on its way to the North Sea – in Mannheim the Neckar, in Mainz the Main, in Koblenz, the Moselle.

The post road ran along the west bank of the river, although the Mozart trail is very cold among the industrial regions and autobahns of the west bank, and is now lost to concrete redevelopment as far as Wörms, where route 9 takes up the course of the old route all the way to Mainz.

Zum König von England was considered to be the best inn in Mainz. It was part of a whole complex of buildings, and was well-known at the time for its inner courtyard, with its carved arcades. It was totally destroyed in the Second World War, and has been redesigned and rebuilt. The inn was situated where the entrance to the Gutenberg Museum now stands, nearly opposite the eastern choir of Mainz Cathedral.

During the course of their week in Mainz, the Mozarts gave a concert at the Romischer König, an inn whose main room was often used as a theatre or concert hall.

The building is still there in the Grebenstrasse, although it has been altered since; it is only about a hundred metres from Zum König von England. The Mozarts had only to cross the eastern part of the market-place and go down a narrow lane, the Liebfrauenstrasse, which joined up with the Grebenstrasse. The building is directly opposite at this point. Before it stands a statue of the mediaeval king from whom it got its name.

Today it is part of the Erbacher Hof, which is a Catholic educational and musical centre, noted for its connection with the Romanian conductor, Sergiu Celibidache. The part of it which was the Romischer König is now the episcopal public library.

During their stay in Mainz, Wolferl met the violinist Karl Michael Esser, on whom he exercised his critical faculties. 'You played well,' he told Esser according to Leopold, recalling the occasion years later, 'but you added too many notes. You ought to play music as it was written.'

According to apocrypha, a similar criticism was made of Wolfgang himself by no less a personage than the Emperor Joseph II of Austria years later, when he complained that there were 'too many notes' in *Die Entführung aus dem Serail.*

What Herr Esser made of Wolferl's comment is not on record.

The Mozarts also met for the first time the soprano Maria Anna de Amicis, who was on her way to London with her father, her sister and her brother. Leopold and Wolferl were to meet – and hear – Maria de Amicis again in Naples and Venice; she also sang the lead in Wolfgang's *Lucio Silla* in Milan in 1772. 'De Amicis is our best friend,' wrote Leopold that year, 'she sings and acts like an angel and is delighted because Wolfgang has served her incomparably.'

On August 10th, the Mozarts left their coach and most of

their luggage at Zum König von England, and went by market boat – a viable alternative to travelling by carriage in the eighteenth century – to Frankfurt, about thirty kilometres upstream along the River Main.

On arrival in Frankfurt, the Mozarts found lodgings at 3 Bendergasse, a building that no longer exists.

Two days after their arrival, there was a heatwave, and Leopold was unable to sleep that night. Being thirsty, he had been drinking the local wines that evening, mixed with mineral water, since he considered the local running water 'awful, tasteless, smelly and opaque.' His condition may well have contributed to his insomnia, and he recorded that he was unable to open the window, as his eyesight would not function as he had wished.

So he amused himself with a mild form of vandalism by scratching graffiti onto the window of his room:

> 'Mozart Maitre de la Musique de la Chapelle de Salzbourg avec sa famille le 12 août 1763,' it said.

The whole pane is now in the possession of the Historical Museum in Frankfurt.

A few days later they moved to Zum Goldenen Löwen, an altogether more prestigious address from which to advertise his concerts. This establishment also no longer exists, although the site, in the Fahrgasse, is marked by a commemorative plaque.

The move paid off, because just a week after their arrival in Frankfurt, the Mozarts gave their first performance. An advertisement ran:

> 'Lovers of music are herewith appraised that on Thursday next, the 18th August at Scharf's Hall on the Liebfrauenberg a concert will be held at 6 o'clock in the evening at which two children, namely a girl of 12 and a boy of 7, will be heard to play with incredible dexterity concertos, trios and sonatas, and then the boy the same on the violin.'

This concert (admission fee – 1 thaler per person) was memorable because it was attended by Frankfurt's most

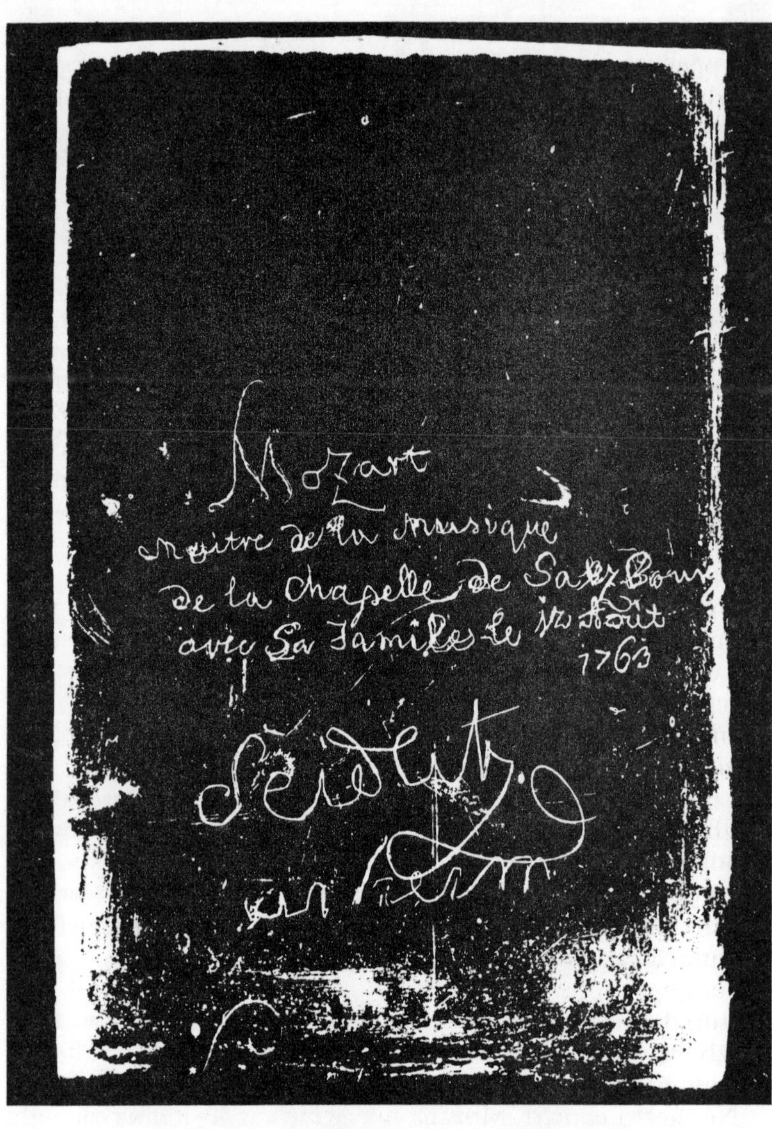

Graffiti scratched onto a windowpane at 3 Bendergasse by Leopold Mozart, now at the Frankfurt Historical Museum.

By courtesy of Historischen Museum, Frankfurt-am-Main.

famous son, Goethe. 'It was when I was 14 years old,' recalled the poet nearly seventy years later. 'I still remember quite clearly the little fellow with his coiffure and his sword.'

The performance was a great success. 'It was very good,' wrote Leopold.

The concerts were repeated on August 22nd, 25th, 26th and 30th. There is no mention of receipts from these concerts, although Leopold writes of some of the gifts received by the children: a fashionable English hat, a snuff-box and embroidery for Nannerl, and a porcelain snuff-box for Wolferl. There was also a letter of recommendation from a wealthy Frankfurt merchant's wife, addressed to Friedrich Melchior Grimm, secretary to the Duc d'Orléans, in Paris. This was a valuable letter, as Grimm was destined to play a very important part in the Mozart story both in the later stages of this tour, and in years to come.

All in all, the tone of Leopold's letters testified to high morale.

'Wolfgang is very jolly, but also a scamp,' wrote Leopold. 'Nannerl now plays so beautifully that she does not suffer by comparison with the boy and everyone admires her execution.'

In the long run, of course, Nannerl did suffer from comparison – who would not beside the genius that was Mozart? Among the talented musicians of the period, one might wonder where Nannerl Mozart might have stood had it not been for her brother. One thing was certain – she was devoted to Wolferl, and there never was a jealous word or an unkind jibe uttered by her. This must testify to a girl of a singular character.

Judging from Leopold's optimistic letters Nannerl had matured and grown in stature since their departure from Salzburg, and Wolferl, did not appear to be suffering unduly at this stage from the trials of touring.

Neither Leopold Mozart nor Thomas Pennant thought much of Frankfurt, although the former wrote that the Romer in the Romerplatz was, 'an altogether beautiful building', while Pennant commented that 'in all Frankfurt there is not a public edifice of any beauty, the town house and the cathedral being very old; the streets in general are ill built.'

At this time Frankfurt was in the throes of a recession because of extensive bankruptcies in Amsterdam and the Netherlands, further down the Rhine, on which Frankfurt's economics largely relied. The Mozarts were to see the effects of these hardships during their visit to the Netherlands in two years' time.

Frankfurt suffered very heavy bombing in the Second World War, and although it has been rebuilt, very little original Mozartiana can now be found. The area where Scharf's Hall was situated has been redeveloped. It used to occupy the vicinity of the Liebfrauenkirche.

The day after the last of the concerts, the Mozarts bade a fond farewell to Frankfurt, and returned to Mainz. Once again, they went by boat, 'for the market boats ply daily between Mainz and Frankfurt.' They reinstalled themselves at the König von England.

This time they stayed for a further fortnight and gave another three concerts, which earned them 200 gulden – a very handsome fortnight's takings.

During their stay in Mainz they visited the Palace of the Elector of Mainz, Emmerich Joseph von Breidtbach in the Rheinstrasse. This baroque Renaissance building was largely destroyed in the Second World War, and its original decoration can only partly be seen today. The Palace is now the Romano-German Museum.

They also went to la Favorite, the Elector's summer residence. This was situated about a mile from the town centre, at the confluence of the Main and the Rhine.

'The country in general along the Main is flat,' wrote Thomas Pennant in 1765 'the river is muddy and not deep, yet has a very gentle course: it falls into the Rhine a little above Mentz (sic), opposite the Chartreuse and la Favorite, the Rhine there is of a great breadth and very rapid.'

At the time of the Mozarts' visit, the Elector was seriously ill, and unable to see them. Leopold, ever the optimistic opportunist, did manage to befriend the Elector's personal valet, Herr Urspringer, a Salzburger by birth. Through him and his family, Leopold was kept informed about the Elector's state of health, and when the rumour spread throughout the city that the Elector had died, Herr Urspringer was able to dispel the rumour.

As usual, Leopold took his family to see several churches, including the Carmelite church in the Karmeliterstrasse, The Augustinerkirche in the Augustinerstrasse, and the Jesuit church of St Ignaz in Kapuzinerstrasse. They also visited the twin onion-domed St Peter's church in the Grosse Bleiche, where Leopold was appalled by the casual and cavalier manner of the mourners at the funeral of an official, as well as by the Cathedral.

On a more secular note, the Mozarts dined with Herr von Dallberg, the music intendant, at his house in the Klara-strasse, which is still preserved today. Leopold came away clutching six bottles of Herr Dallberg's excellent locally produced Hochheimer wine.

The family made several excursions out of town, visiting the environs. Nannerl Mozart noted, in her childishly economical travel diaries, of a trip to the spa town of 'Wisbad' (Wiesbaden), to the north of Mainz. On the way, the Mozarts visited Schloss Biebrich on the Rhine. This was built between 1698 and 1744 as a residence by the Princes and Dukes of Nassau. The Schloss, whose garden and round room were, in Nannerl's eyes, noteworthy, is still there, half way between Mainz and Wiesbaden.

On September 13th Leopold hired a boat, and the Mozarts set off once more on the next stage of the Grand Tour in a different style – through one of the prettiest regions in all Germany.

SCENE SEVEN

Fairy Castles

If there is any part of Germany that embodies the romance of river mythology, it must be the stretch between Mainz and Koblenz, especially from Bingen onwards. Here the Rhine narrows and deepens as it twists and turns among the thickly wooded hills on either side. Here are towns, dominated by historic churches, full of lovely old, half-timbered houses. Here the modern traveller will delight in the ubiquitous castles on the mountain tops, some in ruins, others looking like sets for the fairy tales of the Brothers Grimm, who lived here, and whose legacy lies like an aura over the whole region. Here are the waters where the Rhinemaidens lived, guarding the Rhinegold, upon which Alberich cast the curse that eventually brought down the Gods of Valhalla. Here on the Eastern bank stands the famous echoing Lorelei rock, between Kaub and St Goarshausen, home of the legendary siren said to have lured sailors to their doom.

This is the Germany where the beauties of nature equate with the cursed fatalism that permeates so much of German romantic mythology, from the Bad Fairy in *The Sleeping Beauty* through Goethe's *Faust* to the destruction of Siegfried and Brunhilde.

Unless the traveller wishes to follow literally in the Mozarts' wake, following the route of the old post road would now be the obvious course. The E42 autobahn leaves Mainz on the western bank of the Rhine, and comes off onto route 9 which leads through Bingen, and all the way on to Koblenz, and beyond to Bonn.

The modern traveller would be in a position to drink in this heady atmosphere of gothic fantasy and fatalism to the full, whether from the comforts of a Rhine cruise, or from a car.

To the Mozart children, the trip meant something radically different.

Wolfgang was twenty-nine years old when the first of the Brothers Grimm was born, Goethe was just a lad of fourteen that year, the Lorelei legend was not to be penned until 1800, and Wagner was born twenty-two years after Wolfgang's death.

Instead of conjuring up fairy tales, the ruined castles brought the German curse closer to home. Leopold understood, and no doubt explained to Wolferl and Nannerl some of the hard facts of recent history as shown by the devastation caused by the Thirty Years' War in the first half of the seventeenth century, followed by the French wars in the second half. Although cities like Mainz and Mannheim sparkled with fine, 'modern' buildings, the legacy of the brutalities and religious bigotry of the last hundred years were still very much in evidence in the more provincial parts – like the banks of the Rhine – where reparations were slower in the making.

On the evening of September 17th, the Mozarts disembarked in the city of Koblenz, in the Electorate of Trier, after a four day voyage that was fraught with foul and stormy weather which slowed progress considerably. They passed through Rittersheim (Rudersheim), according to Pennant 'a small town famous for its wine, which is little inferior to that of Hochheim.'

Because of a howling gale, the Mozarts stayed the night at Bingen, before continuing past the Bingenloch. Pennant describes this as 'a rock in the middle of the river, and a slight fall, which makes a little swell in the water . . . and is reputed dangerous.'

> Leopold wrote: 'At midday we came to St Gregoire, where we ate our midday meal, and at two o'clock we started off again but an hour later there was such a storm that we had to stop at a place called Arning. After Arning, with a great deal of trouble, we came to a little place called Salzich, where I booked the best room in the

> house and ordered some food. I therefore had the best room, a soup, a good Rhine salmon and butter.'

Leopold eschewed the inferior local wine in favour of one of the bottles of Hochheimer that Herr von Dallberg had given him in Mainz. A meal to cheer the cockles of the heart on a dark and stormy night!

The Elector of Trier at this time was Archbishop Johann Philip von Walderdorf, one of three Archbishop Electors – the other two being those of Mainz and Cologne. His predecessors had chosen the fortifications of Ehrenbreitstein, overlooking Koblenz, as the electoral seat in preference to the capital, Trier, on the River Moselle, which joins the Rhine in Koblenz. These fortifications date back to 1100, although their present form was established between the sixteenth and eighteenth centuries, and became one of the most important and impenetrable German fortresses in the nineteenth century. Baroque forts and batteries, and an enormous church, were also added to extend Ehrenbreitstein into a very imposing complex.

Below the fortress, on the Rhine, stood the Elector's residence proper, the Kurfürstliche Residenz, known as the Philippsburg, which was built by the Elector Philipp Christian von Soetern between 1626 and 1632. In the second half of the eighteenth century, the Residenz served as a lively intellectual and cultural centre.

Ehrenbreitstein is still there, above the right bank of the Rhine. It is reached either on foot, or by cable car from the bottom of the hill. The view of the city and its confluent rivers is as spectacular now as it was in the eighteenth century.

Remains of the Residenz complex are also there, and its main section is now the Dikasterialgebaude, a fine baroque building set in its own grounds. The Phillippsburg no longer exists.

On their arrival in Koblenz, the Mozarts met Baron von Pergen, the Imperial Envoy, who had arrived at the landing stage at the same time. The Baron had fortuitously attended one of the Mozarts' concerts at Frankfurt a few days previously. They booked into Zu den drei Reichkronen.

This inn was destroyed, and the area redeveloped, but its site is approximately where 2–4 Entempfühl now stands. Over the middle window of the 1st floor is a sign commemorating the stay by Goethe – no mention of Mozart! – on July 15th 1774.

The following day, they once again met Baron von Pergen. He had spoken of the gifted children to the Elector, and now in the company of Baron von Walderndorf had come to take the Mozarts to see the Elector.

'He took my children by the hand and presented them to the Elector.' wrote Leopold, 'which is why we were heard at once.'

On September 18th, therefore, the Mozarts gave a concert at the Philippsburg. In the meantime, the weather settled down, and it merely poured with rain for two days. Wolferl caught a chill, which did not prevent Leopold from arranging a second concert on September 21st for the nobles. It is not known where this concert took place, but, being the cultural centre that it was, the Residenz was the most likely venue.

The day after, Wolferl's chill became worse, and 'on the 22nd in the night turned into catarrh,' recorded Leopold. 'So I must wait for a few days, especially as the weather is so bad.'

Leopold was not always as mindful of his children's health as a father should be, and this was yet another example of Wolfgang having to perform while 'under the weather'.

In the meantime, Leopold continued that, 'we spend most of our time with the family of Baron Kerpen, who is Electoral Privy Councillor and Head of the Nobility, or, according to local speech, Head Knight . . . He has seven sons and two daughters. They all sing and play the violin or violincello, and most also play the clavier.'

While waiting for Wolferl to recover, Leopold took stock of his accounts, and calculated that, since they had left Salzburg, they had spent 1,068 gulden. Considering that his salary at Salzburg was between 300 and 400 gulden per annum, one may elicit some idea of the costings of the Grand Tour so far; although he points out that 'other people have paid for this. We cannot economize because to preserve our health and my court's reputation we must travel nobly and gallantly. We have no other associates but nobles and other distinguished persons, and though I say it myself, our performances bestow great honour to our court.

By September 27th Wolferl had recovered, and the Mozarts continued by boat to Bonn, in the domain of the Archbishop Maximilian Friedrich, Elector of Cologne. As before, the Rhine wound its way among wooded hills and mountains.

SCENE EIGHT

The Unfinished Cathedral

The Mozarts arrived in Bonn that same evening, and put up at the Goldenen Karpfen. This inn was pulled down in the nineteenth century, and the building erected in its place was destroyed in the Second World War. The whole area has now been altered and redeveloped, although the approximate site, at No 24 Rheingasse, is noteworthy for a curious quirk of fate. Next door, at No 26, stands an hotel named after one of Mozart's most eminent pupils of later years, and Bonn's most famous son: Hotel Beethoven.

The Elector was away at the time, so Leopold saw no reason to linger in the Electorate of Cologne for longer than was necessary. In his diary Leopold mentions some of the sights of Bonn.

The most impressive building was the Elector's palace, the Schloss, originally built in the thirteenth century, but reconstructed in the baroque style by the Elector Joseph Clemens between 1697 and 1702. In 1777 it was largely destroyed by fire, and all its fittings were consumed by flames; in 1818 the building was taken over by the Rheinische Landesuniversität. It was also severely damaged in the Second World War, but has been rebuilt, and now houses the University.

Schloss Poppelsdorf, an annexe of the Electoral residence became the Botanical Gardens in the nineteenth century. It was also badly bombed and partly rebuilt after the Second World War. Today it too is part of the University complex.

The most curious site, however, was probably the baroque Kreuzburg pilgrimage church at Poppelsdorf. Its main feature is the Holy Staircase, by which Leopold the devout Catholic must have been very affected. To climb up, pilgrims must do so on their knees; only at the edges can they walk up or down. This church is still there.

The Mozarts also managed to see the superb Baroque Town Hall, dating from 1738, before continuing on their way, this time by hired carriage, towards Brühl.

The modern traveller would doubtless add the Beethovenhaus at 20 Bonnstrasse to their itinerary, as well as the Old Cemetery in Bornheimer Strasse, where Robert and Clara Schuman are buried.

At lunchtime, the coach pulled up outside the Englischen Grüss Inn. According to Leopold a good place 'to rest one's feet and feed one's horses.'

Falkenlust was a hunting lodge, completed in 1740, that had originally belonged to the Elector Clemens August (1723–1761). It is still there. Both Leopold and Nannerl were particularly struck by the Mirror Room and the Chinese Room. In the grounds of Falkenlust they walked down the Allee to the Pheasantry, and visited the Indian House as well as the so-called Snail House by the Canal.

After this they visited the Elector's country seat in Brühl, Schloss Augustusberg, and its extensive gardens. This imposing rococo building, one of the finest of its kind, was begun in 1725 and completed by Cuvilliés in 1770. It boasts an elegant staircase by Balthasar Neumann, along which hung the portraits of five Bavarian Electors, which Leopold saw fit for special mention in his diary.

After lunch, the coach continued on its way, and the Mozarts reached Cologne that evening at a reasonable hour. They stayed at the Heilige Geist – where Goethe also stayed in 1774. This inn was pulled down in the ninteenth century, and during the Second World War the whole area was totally destroyed. Redevelopment altered the topography completely, and the site is now virtually untraceable.

'Cologne is very old and very big and we stayed there two days,' wrote Leopold. 'We had the opportunity to see the treasure and all the holy places in the Minster.'

The Cathedral of St Peter and St Mary is one of the finest examples of German gothic architecture, with a foundation stone dating back to 1248, although the whole Cathedral was not fully completed until it was consecrated in the presence of Kaiser Wilhelm I in 1880. It was, at the time, the highest structure in the world, and one of the largest churches in Christendom. Among its treasures mentioned by Leopold is the Reliquary of the Three Kings, which is now situated behind the High Altar.

The Mozarts saw only an unfinished cathedral, which had stood half-built for five centuries. Leopold was singularly unimpressed with it:

> 'I went there with my family and two canons of Bamberg and Mainz, and I was very annoyed when the Custodian who was supposed to show us the treasure came to Vespers drunk. The Cathedral is so loathsome it is impossible to describe it. Inside are four church pews made out of two long, round bits of wood nailed together, more like a field chapel. In a corner straw chairs that could be hired lay together in a heap. Half way up stands a horrible, ancient walnut-brown painted pulpit on four feet, of which one is broken and two people can carry it back and forth. On this pulpit Luther had to preach, and if he were here today he would have to use the same pulpit. Nearby stand two old chests supported by two pillars. The chests look as if they will fall apart any minute. The choir is locked up and to get to the high altar one must go through a pair of side chapels or else look through a window. The psalter is more of the Jewish school than Christian singing, and the boys that sang the Antiphon seemed to have something in their mouths. They sang absolutely nothing, in fact they shrieked like street Arabs in full-throat when they are fooling about.'

Leopold was, however, very interested in the Jesuit Church of St Maria Himmelfahrt in the Marzellenstrasse, since one of its features was a pulpit sculpted by Geisselbrünn of Augsburg in 1634.

Leopold the relic seeker was also drawn to the church of St Ursula on Ursulaplatz, which contained not only the remains of the virgin martyr herself, but also a proportion of a reputed 11,000 other virgins as well. Thomas Pennant wrote that, 'most of the skulls are adorned with pearls. On a scaffolding consisting of some dozens of benches are ranged hundreds of skulls of St Ursula's companions of the lower rank; and, above, the walls are closely covered with their bones.'

Today, the walls of the Goldene Kammer are full of reliquary niches, and human bones are arranged to form various symbols and inscriptions.

Pennant went on to write that, 'here I was shown a large alabaster jar, one that served at the marriage at Canaan. A priest exhibits all this and has half a crown for his trouble.'

There is a wry legend, put about by the Germans, that of the twelve apostles, eighteen of them are buried in Germany.

Cologne was a large city, and despite the gardens and vineyards within its walls, Pennant commented that 'its streets are narrow, very dirty even to be offensive to the smell and very ill built. It has no manufacture and abounds with religious and beggars.' He added that there were fourteen convents, thirty-seven nunneries, twenty-one parish churches, eleven collegiate churches and two abbey churches, serving a community of some 30,000 souls.

After the Mozart's two day stay, it was time to leave behind the mighty river Rhine that had been their almost constant companion ever since Mannheim.

'From Cologne we went by mail coach to Aachen,' wrote Leopold. The coach passed under the Hahnentor, which is still there, out of Cologne and on to the open road. 'It was a dreadful road,' added Leopold.

SCENE NINE

Windchimes

One of the criticisms levelled at Leopold concerning his taking Wolfgang and Nannerl on long tours round Europe was that they missed out on their education. Whereas this was true in one sense, there was no doubt that Leopold, himself a cultured and educated man, drew extensively on the University of the Road to teach his children everything they needed to know. Travel, as is endlessly pointed out, broadens the mind. Whether or not Leopold put his children through too much – or not enough – is debatable, for, although there is much evidence of the Mozarts having visited churches, cathedrals and courts, there is no mention of what the children did by way of recreation. It is true that there are references to Nannerl's interest in fashions, especially foreign styles, and that Wolferl was generally a sparkling, fun-loving boy, but one might wonder if they owned any dolls or toys, apart from toothpicks and snuff-boxes.

There was always Rücken, of course, but was it just creative mental play, a bit of fun, or was Rücken an escape from Leopold's high intellectual, religious and cultural standards? After all, how much intellectualism, religion and culture can a seven year old take?

Even among discerning adults, the time sometimes comes when the mind becomes saturated, and one gothic cathedral begins to resemble another, and all Dutch paintings begin to merge in the mind. Leopold, as we know, always made a point of going first to see the cathedral, or main church, of every new place that the Mozarts arrived at, if only to see the organ.

Was Wolfgang possibly introduced to too many cathedrals in too concentrated a time span? One cannot comment on his taste for architecture, for no relevant documentation exists; but his life-long love for the organ as the king of all instruments is well established.

On the evening of September 30th, the Mozarts passed through the Kölntor – today the Hansemann-Platz – of the fashionable spa town of Aachen, or Aix-la-Chappelle, having stopped in Lovenich, Bergheim, the staging posts in the market places of Jülich, Aldenhoven, Broichweiden, and the Alte Haus in the Steinweg in Haaren. Route 55 from Cologne to Jülich, and route 1 from Jülich to Aachen is the old post route as it is today.

They booked in at the Goldenen Drachen, an extremely reputable – and expensive – hotel in the Komphausbadstrasse, catering mostly for the rich and famous.

That night, Leopold suffered a severe attack of gout, and found himself barely able to function. The following day, therefore, he did not visit Aachen's famous Cathedral, as one might have expected. The Cathedral, in the Münster Platz, dates back to the ninth century, is the resting place of Charlemagne, and contains his hunting horn as well as his throne. Leopold would certainly have taken his children to see the cathedral, and given them a history lesson about one of France's greatest legends, had he been fit to do so.

In Aachen Wolferl had his first taste of a totally different kind of music, a sound peculiar to the Netherlands – that of the carillon in its simplest form. Burney recounts that in the streets of Aachen there were hung 'a great number of oblong pieces of glass, cut and tuned in such a manner, as to form little peals of four or five bells, all in the same key, which were played on by the wind.'

Today, windchimes are a common and delightful decoration, and cheap gift shops are full of them; but these Dutch gimmicks must have given great delight to Wolferl and Nannerl when they heard their tinkling tones for the very first time.

The day after their arrival, the Mozarts met, and played for, Princess Amalie, the youngest sister of King Frederick the Great of Prussia. Anna Amalie Hohenzollern was born in Berlin in 1723, and died there in 1787. The youngest child of Frederick William I and Sophie Dorothea of the House of Hanover, she was an ardent lover of music, and was trained by her brother – himself a flautist, composer and musician of some considerable repute – and Gottlieb Hayne, cathedral organist in Berlin. She became a very proficient harpsicord player and music played a very important part in her life and in her court. C.P.E. Bach was one of her kappellmeisters. A conservative composer with conservative tastes, who wrote a number of flute sonatas, her most ambitious composition was a Passion entitled *Of Jesus' Death.* She was a keen collector of music, and her collection included over a hundred titles by J.S Bach, held in the Prussian Royal Library.

Amalie never married, and spent most of her life in Berlin. She gambled heavily and was deeply in debt all her life, relying on 'Old Fritz', as her illustrious brother was affectionately known, to bail her out.

Until the Peace of Hubertsburg in 1748, Aachen had virtually been a war zone, victim of the French wars and the War of the Austrian Succession, and it was only now that the town had recovered enough to throw its doors open to the titled and the wealthy of Europe to take its waters. In 1763, illness prompted Princess Amalie, accompanied by a host of physicians, to be among the first of the fashionable set to come to Aachen. She had taken a house near the Goldenen Drachen for the duration.

Being a music lover, the Princess jumped at the opportunity to hear the Mozarts performing, and promptly arranged for them to give a concert that same day. The concert probably took place on the first floor of the Alte Redoute, next door to the Goldenen Drachen – possibly since the room was the only venue large enough for a concert. It is also likely that Leopold's gout did not prevent him from selling tickets at the door!

The Princess was overwhelmed by the Mozarts and could not enthuse enough about Wolferl and his sister, whose performance she remunerated with hugs and kisses – but no 'present'. She even suggested that the Mozarts should come to Berlin, an invitation that Leopold politely declined, since – 'she herself has no money. If the kisses she gave to my children, and especially Master Wolfgang were really louis d'or, we would have been lucky enough. But neither landlords nor postmasters are paid in kisses.'

Leopold went on to add tantalizingly that, 'she made a proposition to me which I shall not write down here, as nobody would believe it, I did not believe it myself what she suggested to me!'

Leopold did not trust Princess Amalie, and he cryptically penned the opening of a quotation from Horace with which no doubt his friend Hagenauer was familiar – *Vestigia terrent.* The full quotation being, 'The wary fox in the fable answered the sick lion: Because I am frightened by the footprints. I see them all pointing towards your den. None of them point away.'

Which, presumably, suggested to Leopold that the time was ripe to move on, particularly since Aachen was 'the most expensive place that I have met during our journey.'

Today, nothing is left of the Komphausbadstrasse or any of the buildings in it. The whole topography of Aachen has now been radically altered.

SCENE TEN

The Iron Monkey

The next day, on October 2nd and seventy-five gulden lighter, the Mozarts set off once more by post coach, through the Jakobstor, towards Liège. 'From Aachen we went to Lüttich [Liège] where we arrived at nine o'clock at night as the iron hoop on our wheel fell off. Lüttich is big, populous and productive.'

They spent one night at l'Aigle Noire, reputedly one of the finest – and no doubt most expensive – hostelries in Europe, which counted among its illustrious guests King George IV of England, the Comte d'Artois – the brother of Louis XVI of France, King Louis XVIII, and Field Marshal Blücher, as well as members of the Austrian Imperial Family and the House of Orange. The establishment no longer exists, but was situated in the rue Feronstrée near the Pont St Léonard close to the north bank of the Meuse, at approximately where Nos 19–23 now stand.

The following day the Mozarts set off once more along the straight, paved road towards Brussels.

'From Liège to Paris,' wrote Leopold, 'the post road is paved as in a town, and on either side it is planted with trees like a garden path.'

What a familiar sounding description of a modern French road! Unfortunately, this same road wrought havoc with the wheels, since once again, the iron hoop of one of the other wheels fell off.

> 'We had to wait till the wheel was repaired, so we took our midday lunch in a horrible place which was an inn where only travellers ate. We were seated on straw chairs by the open fire where a

> cauldron hung on a long chain, in which meat, turnips, carrots etc. were seething all together. We sat at a miserable little table and we were served out of the great cauldron with soup and meat, and a bottle of red Champagne was brought out; but not a word of German was spoken, only pure Walloon, that is, bad French. The door was left open and for that reason we often had the honour of pigs grunting around us, and hens paid us a visit.'

The night of October 3rd saw the Mozarts at Tirlemont, where they booked in at the Tiennen Schotel in the town square. This hotel was also one of the best and smartest hostelries in the region, and recorded Napoleon, the Duke of Wellington, Field Marshal Blücher, Frederick Wilhelm III of Prussia, and the Romanovs among its eminent patrons. Still in existence, the building is now the Music Academy and Cultural Centre, and is one of Tirlemont's most important historical buildings.

Leopold found Tirlemont interesting, and commented on the legacy of war that he saw there: 'Tirlemont must in its time have been an excellent fortress; it is sad to see the destroyed ramparts, walls, gates and the fine outer works. In the centre it has a very fine square such as one does not find in many much larger towns.'

The following day the Mozarts made good progress, and reached Louvain in time to attend mass at the 'principal church. The beautiful marble altars and precious paintings of the famous Netherlands' artists begin here. I was transfixed by a LAST SUPPER,' wrote Leopold.

The church in question is St Peter's and the painting is the tryptich by Dierick Bouts, circa 1464. Leopold commented further on its altars of 'beautiful black and white marble, also many striking old paintings.'

Today, part of the church is partitioned off, and serves as a museum, where some fine Dutch paintings, including the 'Last Supper', can be viewed.

Emerging from the church, the Mozarts could not help seeing what Leopold referred to as the 'beautiful town hall' just opposite, before going round the corner to lunch at the

The "Tiennenschotel" in Tirlemont, in eighteenth century and today.

By courtesy of Harrie Spellmans.

excellent Wildeman Inn, where they were very well treated. The Wildeman Inn is no longer there, but in its place stands the Palace of Justice, in the Ferdinand Smoldersplein. This is just off the Jodenstraat, which makes up one side of the Cathedral square.

That same evening, the Mozarts arrived for a six-week stay in Brussels, where they were lodged at the Hôtel d'Angleterre. This fine hotel used to be situated on the corner of rue de la Madeleine and Cantersteen. It was pulled down in 1937, and on its site the central railway station was built.

In 1763, the area which is very approximately what is now Belgium as well as a chunk of northern France, constituted the Austrian Netherlands, which meant that the Mozarts were in effect politically on home ground. The Austrian Netherlands were governed by Prince Charles of Lorraine, the brother of the Austrian Emperor Francis I, for whom the Mozarts had played just over a year previously in Vienna.

The Prince's palace in Brussels was a large building with a square in the middle. It commanded a fine view of both the city and the surrounding countryside. The appartments were lavishly furnished with artefacts and objects d'art, including exquisite Dutch tapestries, black Chinese lacquerwork, and life sized, correctly dressed figures, delicate porcelain, Flemish paintings, and Japanese bowls.

'His Highness' laboratory has a collection of the different instruments used by watchmakers, one a great machine,' wrote Thomas Pennant, testifying to the Prince's interest not only in the arts, but also in technology. 'There is a stove for hatching chickens and some other stoves for chymical (sic) experiments.'

Leopold, overwhelmed by the sheer size of the Prince's collection, wrote 'I found therein an indescribable amount of all kinds of natural history specimens. I have seen many such collections but none in such quantity and of so many different sorts.'

Charles of Lorraine's palace was partially demolished, and has been rebuilt; the site today is where the Bibliothèque Royale Albert Ier, and the musée d'Arts ancien et moderne stand, in the Place Royale.

Prince Charles was an enlightened governor, who built

roads and waterways, and contributed greatly to the growth and development of agriculture in the province, and encouraged industry and enterprise.

Leopold recorded a different opinion, saying that 'his present recreations are to lacquer, paint, varnish, eat, drink and laugh so loud that one can hear him 3 or 4 rooms away.' The real reason for this low opinion was that, having agreed to listen to the children, Prince Charles kept putting them off.

'You must await my decision,' the Prince told Leopold.

The delay infuriated Leopold, who complained bitterly, 'I shall also have a mighty bill to pay at the hotel.'

In the meantime, the Mozarts busied themselves meeting and playing for a variety of people in their homes, including Archbishop Frankenberg of Malines (Mechelen) – of whom more later, and General Count de Ferraris. They were befriended by Count Coronini who called on them daily and introduced them to Brussels society. The children were showered with presents: Nannerl was given Dutch lace by the Archbishop, as well as pretty coats and cloaks from various courtiers, while Wolferl received two impressive swords.

'With snuff boxes and étuis and such stuff,' wrote Leopold wrily, 'we could furnish a stall.'

By the end of the Grand Tour, the Mozart children had collected nine gold watches, twelve gold snuff-boxes, earings, necklaces, knives – including a fruit-knife with one gold and one silver blade, toothpicks and toothpick boxes and swords – to the value of 12,000 gulden! On these calculations, Leopold's stall would have brought in thirty-five times his annual salary in Salzburg.

Leopold also took advantage of the time on his hands by looking round the churches, including the Great and Little Carmelite churches, the Jesuit church, and, of course, the Cathedral. Everywhere he saw and admired the black and white marble that so typified Flemish church architecture. Of the paintings he singled out for special mention Ruben's *Our Saviour Delivering The Keys To St Peter*, which he saw in the Chapel of the Holy Sacrament at the Cathedral. Leopold was in awe of the Flemish masters, and listed many whose paintings he had seen in Brussels, including: 'Hubert and

St Peter's Church, Louvain, where Leopold Mozart admired the *Last Supper* by Dierick Bouts.

Source: Zaluski photograph.

Hans van Eyck, Pieter Paul Rubens, Jacob Jordans, Paul Brill, Antonius van Dyck and Rembrant van Ryn.'

On a more secular note, Leopold waxed eloquent about the city. 'Brussels is a beautiful town, the best I have seen,' he wrote. 'The pavements are perfect, the houses very fine, the streets long and bright and the town is lit up at night. The Canal which goes to Holland through Mechelin and Antwerp is the cause of the flourishing trade here, and is a most admirable Canal to be seen with the great Dutch boats with two or three tall masts, full of people. The Canal is enclosed in a stone wall with pillars on each side where lanterns, which are lit up at night, hang.'

The Mozarts also walked on the Ramparts, from which they could see the whole city spread out beneath them, and Nannerl, the fashion-conscious girl that she was, recorded the promenade where the city's fashionable beaux and dandies desported themselves.

After five weeks, Prince Charles found time between 'hunting, eating and drinking' to hear the Mozarts. The Prince was not in fact a music lover, but did play the oboe – as well as the water harmonica. So, by coincidence, did Wolfgang, so Prince and Prodigy struck common ground over a glass immediately! Wolfgang even wrote for this curious device in later years. Consequently, Leopold recorded that 'a fine concert was held, at which Prince Charles was present.'

The concert, on November 14th, almost certainly took place at the palace. One of the pieces performed was a *Sonata in C for piano and violin, K6,* the allegro of which Wolfgang wrote in Brussels at this time.

'I shall plunder some fat thalers and louis d'or,' wrote Leopold in anticipation.

On November 15th the Hôtel d'Angleterre was duly paid their 'mighty bill', no doubt in fat thalers and louis d'or, and the Mozarts set off once more for Paris.

The journey was not without its traumas. Leopold wrote:

> 'We did a post station every hour, firstly because there was not much post and also because we went at full gallop. The journey from Brussels to Paris was very expensive. The post from Brussels to

> Valenciennes was Flemish, and each horse cost us 45 kreuzer. To go to Valenciennes one must take 6 horses, and there is no option but to pay. One has to have 2 postilions who are changed at each station. As they dress according to their own choice I thought it was a pair of rat-catchers, then a pair of villains from a farce, then a pair of ass-drovers, then a pair of ex-hairdressers or unemployed valets, and then a pair of field sergeants. These people drove as though we were the state army pursued by the Prussians. One had enough to worry about so one tipped them so that they would not spring the wheels, and would check the baggage at each post station to make sure it was properly tied on.'

That evening, they arrived at Mons, the birthplace and home of Orlando di Lasso, and stayed the night.

Built into the wall at the entrance to the Stadhuis is a small, iron monkey, dating back to the fifteenth century, called the 'Grande Garde'. Legend has it that whosoever strokes the monkey's head will enjoy good luck. Did little Wolferl make use of this device? Was he even aware that it existed? One would like to think that he did!

While in Mons the Mozarts called on some friends from Vienna before continuing across the flat Flemish countryside to Peronne, the last town before the French border, where they spent their final night on Austrian territory.

Like in all frontier towns, the customs officers were ruthless. Thomas Pennant was there the following year, and recorded that: 'at the gates [of Peronne] I was most strictly searched; and such part of my luggage as was not plombe, and also the whole chaise was thoroughly rummaged.' Presumably the Mozarts' treasure chest of swords, snuff boxes and toothpicks came through unscathed!

After Peronne, the coach crossed the French frontier, and the Mozarts stopped for one final night in Gournay, before the post coach passed through the Porte de la Villette, and finally pulled up, on the afternoon of November 18th, in the courtyard of the Hôtel Beauvais in Paris.

The post route from Brussels is now the N6 to Mons.

There it becomes the N51 Valenciennes road, which leads across today's border into France, where the road number changes to the N30. This continues through Valenciennes to Cambrai.

At Cambrai the road changes to the N44 going south towards St Quentin, but after ten kilometres it turns right and becomes the D917 to Peronne. Here it meets up with the N17, which leads past le Bourget Airport, and along the final stretch of the N2 straight into Paris.

ACT
2

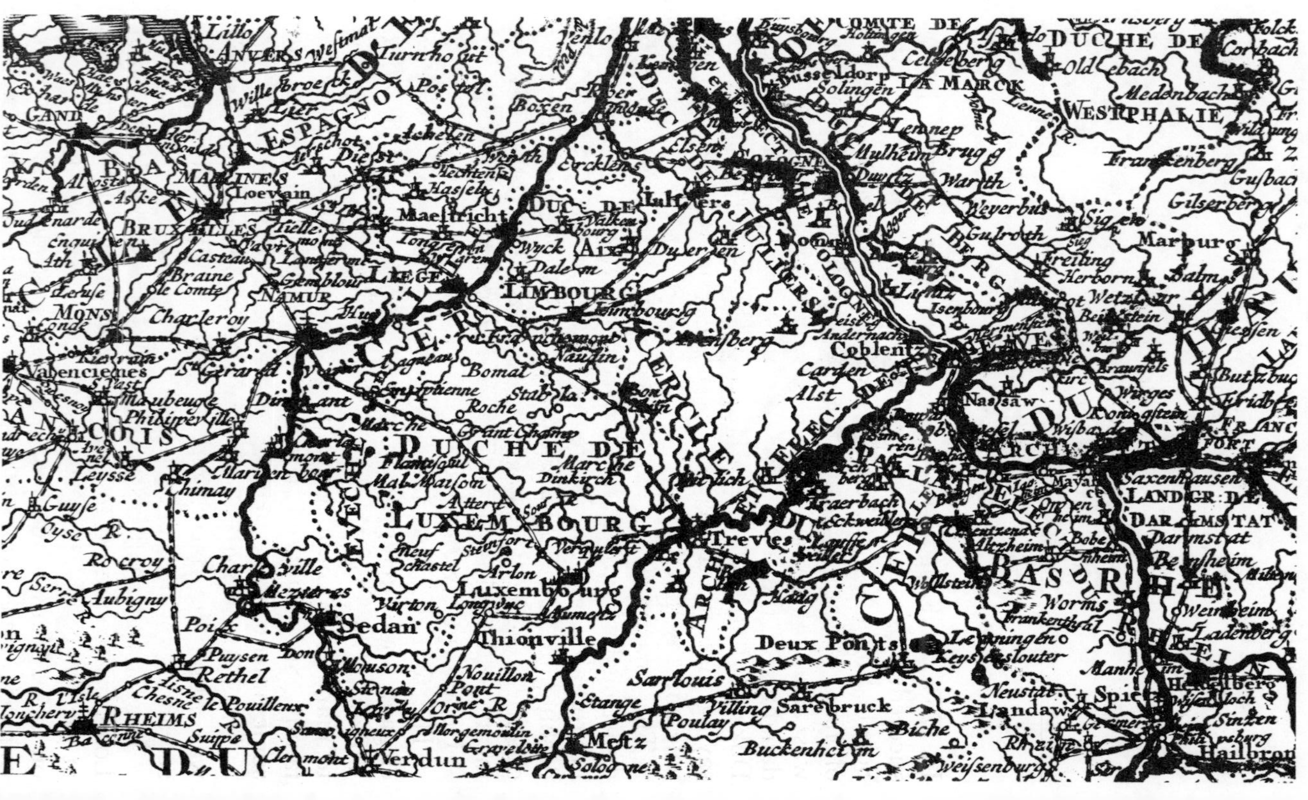

ANVERS
ESPAGNOL
BRUXELLES
MALINES
Maestricht
LIEGE
NAMUR
Charleroy
MONS
LIMBOURG
JULIERS
COLOGNE
Dusseldorp
LA MARCK
WESTPHALIE
Marburg
Coblentz
CERCLE
DUCHE DE
LUXEMBOURG
Luxembourg
Treves
Thionville
Sedan
Charleville
Rethel
RHEIMS
Verdun
Metz
Sarlouis
Sarebruck
Deux Ponts
Worms
Darmstat
Landaw
Heidelberg
Hailbron

PRELUDE

In 1763, the King of France was Louis XV (1710–74), who succeeded his great grandfather, Louis XIV, the 'Roi Soleil'. Louis XV acceded to the throne of France at the age of five. When he came of age at thirteen, a marriage was arranged to the dull and dowdy Maria Leszczyńska, daughter of the adventure-scarred ex-King of Poland and Duke of Lorraine, Stanislas Leszczyński (once quoted as saying that, 'the two most boring queens in Europe are my wife and my daughter').

The marriage, in 1725, had been arranged by the disastrously inept Duke of Bourbon. It was a politically unprofitable match. Louis XV himself was a handsome, dashing man, but weak-willed and lacking in leadership qualities. Nevertheless, both politically and personally, he meant well, and treated his queen politely and kindly.

He also ran two noted mistresses.

The first of these was Mme de Pompadour, a shrewd, elegant and intelligent woman. She was also a friend of Voltaire. She read the king's weaknesses well and was able to manipulate them to her own advantage and that of her family. She exercised a great deal of political power with some drastic consequences for France.

The second mistress, who was yet to appear on the scene, was Mme du Barry, who eventually died, fighting and screaming for mercy, on the guillotine in 1793.

Having inherited his great grandfather's political system, Louis had continued to surround himself with the aristocracy at the Palace of Versailles, where he was able to keep an eye on them. Many of them actually had apartments in the palace complex, while others had town houses in the capital. The road from Paris to Versailles was a never-ending clatter of luxurious carriages commuting constantly back and forth.

The ploy may have been necessary during certain periods in the past, but was now not only futile, but positively harmful to the French economy, still reeling from the aftermath of the Seven Years' War. Apart from having degenerated into what could only be described as a never-ending house party, it resulted in numerous estates going to rack and ruin with no one to run them, causing agriculture and provincial life to go into a steep decline, resulting in hardship and famine. The most fertile country in Europe was unable to feed itself.

Louis nevertheless ruled from a capital city that was the hub of Europe. French was the European lingua franca, and was spoken as a matter of course by courtiers and diplomats in all the best salons between Paris and St Petersburg.

The royal palace of Versailles was copied throughout Europe: Schönbrunn in Vienna, the Arsenal in Berlin, Sans Souci (even the name is French), Frederick the Great's palace in Potsdam, and the University of Vienna, all owe a considerable debt to the Roi Soleil's vision of elegant splendour.

On the surface, the situation seemed stable, vital and alive, although beneath the glossy surface, in the filthy, muddy open sewers that were the streets of downtown Paris, and in the crumbling, neglected provinces, already the seeds of the impending Revolution were germinating. Not only politically, but also intellectually: for the Age of Enlightenment had arrived as well, even though Voltaire and Rousseau, who were in the vanguard of the movement, were no longer living in Paris, and the Arts – with the exception of Music – were in a dull and stagnant state.

Church and army posts were only available to those of noble birth, to the resentment of the growing bourgeoisie. The peasants and slum-dwellers, downtrodden, hungry and neglected, with no hope whatsoever of advancement, were ripe for stirring up.

Leopold Mozart recognized the French salon as a melting pot of ideas, conversation, music, art, fashion and literature. His own interest, however, lay in stirring up accolades for Nannerl and Wolferl.

SCENE ONE

At the Court of Versailles

In the 18th century the rue St Antoine was a long, straight road, longer than it is today. It bustled with merchants and beggars, and was flanked by fine, comfortable houses occupied by the middle and diplomatic classes. The eastern end of it was dominated by the imposing and seemingly impenetrable fortress prison, the Bastille. Surrounding it was the maze of filthy, narrow, souk-like streets which made pre-Revolutionary Paris look like a vastly extended, higgledy-piggledy village, with very little planning evident. In 1763, Count van Eyck, the Bavarian ambassador to Paris, was renting an apartment in the enormous and prestigious Hotel Beauvais, in the rue St Antoine. His wife was the daughter of Count Georg Anton Felix Arco, the Salzburg Chamberlain, whom Leopold knew well.

At Leopold's instigation, Rosalie Joli, Count Arco's chambermaid, had managed to arrange accomodation for the Mozarts with the van Eycks; decent rooms were very scarce in Paris, due to the inordinate influx of English visitors, for whom Paris was the fashionable place to go to that year.

The van Eycks greeted them with open arms when they arrived on the afternoon of November 18th. The Countess, especially, welcomed them hospitably. 'They were very friendly towards us and arranged for a room where we are living comfortably and well,' wrote Leopold. And cheaply. It cost only 100 livres, about £4, per month.

The Countess also gave them her own clavier to use during their stay.

The Hotel Beauvais is still there, at No 68 in what is now the rue François Miron in the 4th Arrondissement, an area

The "Hotel Beauvais" in rue St. Antoine, Paris. Where the Mozart family stayed.

By courtesy of Musée Carnavalet, Paris.

known as the Marais. The hotel had until recently a strong tradition of music, and was the venue of the annual Festival of the Marais, with regular concerts held in the courtyard. Today, the magnificent building stands empty and derelict, its structure unsafe. At the time of writing, the hotel's future is uncertain, with various bodies trying to find ways of preventing its demolition, preserving it and restoring it to its former glory.

Countess van Eyck doted shamelessly on Wolferl.

'Wolfgang loves the Countess, and she loves him in return,' wrote Leopold.

He had arrived in Paris with a portfolio full of letters of recommendation to various people, none of which turned out to be of any use except for one, written by the wife of a merchant whom he had met in Frankfurt. It was addressed to M. Friedrich Melchior Grimm. 'This M. Grimm is my great friend,' wrote Leopold. 'He is Secretary to the Duc d'Orléans, and is a learned man and a great humanitarian. All my other letters and recommendations were useless, even those from the French Ambassador in Vienna, the Imperial Ambassador in Paris and all the letters of introduction from our Minister in Brussels, Count Cobenzl, Prince Conti, Duchesse d'Aiguillon and all the others, wherein I could write a Litany.'

Friedrich Grimm was to become one of the major factors in the Mozart story, especially as far as Wolfgang's sojourns in Paris were concerned. He was born in Regensburg in 1723, the son of a pastor, and went on to study in Leipzig and Paris, where he consequently chose to live. He secured the post of secretary to Louis-Phillippe, Duke of Chartres and Orléans (1725-85), a cousin of King Louis XV. The Duke, among his many other interests, was very fond of the theatre, so Grimm was able to exert considerable influence on the literary and cultural life of Paris.

He was the founder of the literary newsletter, the *Correspondance Littéraire*, in which he informed the courts of Europe of all the latest political, cultural and diplomatic news. He was also *au fait* with all the latest literary trends, and counted such notables as Rousseau, Voltaire, d'Alembert and Diderot among his circle of friends.

Besides, he was a shrewd businessman, knew how to pull strings, and was visionary enough to realize that the Mozart family were more than a mere travelling troupe of musicians from the backwaters of provincial Austria. He was in a position to introduce the Mozarts into Paris' salons, and by the second week in December, the children were already enchanting French society with their prowess. Their reputation gradually spread throughout the capital, and in the weeks approaching Christmas, they had played in many private houses, and received many 'presents'.

Grimm was well connected, knew Mme de Pompadour, and had managed to arrange for the Mozarts to be

Detail from the tomb of the Infanta Isabella of Parma, in the Habsburg Vaults in the Augustinerkirche, Vienna.

Source: Załuski photograph.

presented at court. But not before Christmas.

The delay was because Versailles had been in mourning for the Infanta Isabella of Parma, the King's granddaughter. She had died of smallpox on November 27th.

Isabella's mother was one of Louis XV's twin daughters, Marie-Louise, and her father was the second son of King Philip V of Spain – hence the title of Infanta.

There was actually a strong Mozart connection in the event. When the Mozarts were at the Austrian court in Vienna the previous year, the Emperor Francis I invited Leopold, in his capacity as expert on violin playing and author of *Violinschule*, to go and hear the twenty-one year old Infanta Isabella play the violin.

At the time, Isabella had been married for two years to the Emperor's eldest son and heir, the Archduke Joseph, who was the same age as the Infanta. By all accounts, the young couple were ideally matched, and Joseph loved her very much.

There is a painting of Isabella hanging in the Archduke Franz Karl's salon at Schönbrunn.

Whether or not Leopold appreciated the Infanta's violin playing is not documented, but he would have been upset at hearing of her death at this time, one year later.

One year later still, in 1765, the Archduke succeeded his father as the Emperor Joseph II, and remarried, albeit unhappily. He was to radically affect the Mozart story in later years.

The Mozarts travelled down to Versailles on Christmas Eve, and booked in at Au Cormier, in the rue des Bons Enfants. This establishment no longer exists, and the road has been renamed rue du Peintre Lebrun. It is only a matter of yards from the Royal Chapel of Versailles. The site of the inn today is occupied by Nos 4–6, a small apartment block best seen from round the corner in the rue Colbert, from the courtyard of 'Les Trois Marches', a restaurant of some considerable repute. The site of Au Cormier is the building at the back of the courtyard.

When the Mozarts arrived at Versailles on Christmas Eve, their reputation had preceded them, and they were received with considerable interest by the remarkable Mme de Pompadour.

King Louis's mistress was born Jeanne Antoinette Poisson in 1745, and rose to become a driving force behind the throne of France, and tone setter for the court. She had been in her time, a very striking woman, not beautiful, but certainly elegant, charming and intelligent. She was, at this time, past her prime and suffering from the consumption from which she was to die during the coming year.

Wolferl took a positive dislike to her. The fact that she had him placed on a table in order to inspect him as one would inspect an interesting specimen may have clouded his judgment as well, but he overlooked the matter at first, and was quite prepared to give her the benefit of the doubt. But the final straw came when the friendly and affectionate little boy tried to kiss her.

Mme de Pompadour recoiled.

This upset Wolferl considerably, and, forgetting his protocol, he asked in a voice that the King's mistress could hear, 'Who is this woman who will not kiss me? Why, the Empress herself kissed me!'

Although this remark was noted by Leopold, who most probably cringed with horror at the time, Mme de Pompadour's reaction is not on record. Leopold had contradictory opinions about Mme de Pompadour. 'She is very haughty,' he wrote on the one hand, 'and still rules over everything.'

In a later letter, however, his opinion is more tempered and objective: 'She must have been beautiful, for she is still pretty. She is a fine-looking person, fat, or well-bodied, however well proportioned, blond . . . with eyes like the Empress. She is very proud and uncommonly intelligent.'

It is certain, if not actually documented, that Wolfgang played for Mme de Pompadour, either in Versailles or at her Paris residence, which is now the Elysée Palace. Leopold wrote that: 'her apartments at Versailles are like a paradise and look on the gardens,' and describes, 'the room where the clavecin is – which is all gilt and most unusually lacquered and painted.'

Mme de Pompadour would certainly not have summoned a musical prodigy of repute just to stand him on a table and inspect him, especially since there was a clavier in the apartment, so we may safely speculate that Wolfgang played for her.

During their stay in Versailles, the Mozarts attended the Royal Masses every day, arriving at the Royal Chapel by sedan chairs. It was not done to arrive at court on foot, even though their lodgings were only a few yards away. Besides, the weather was cold, wet and miserable, and the rain used to play havoc with hair which had been carefully coiffured by Sebastian Winter to make it fit for court appearance. Also they all had the new black clothes bought in Paris for wearing at court, which Leopold did not want exposed to the mercy of the elements. This constant use of sedan chairs, and the need to buy new clothes, caused Leopold to complain about the expenses of the Versailles stay.

Meanwhile, they continued to give private concerts in noble houses.

On New Year's Day, the Mozarts presented themselves at the court of Versailles.

Horace Walpole was in Paris and Versailles in 1765, and was also presented at court. He wrote:

> 'The Queen took great notice of me, none of the rest said a syllable. You are let into the King's bedchamber just as he has put on his shirt; he dresses and talks good-humouredly to a few, glares at strangers, goes to mass, to dinner, and a-hunting. The good old Queen . . . is at the dressing table, attended by two or three old ladies, who are languishing to be in Abraham's bosom, as the only man's bosom to whom they can hope for admittance. Thence you go to the Dauphin, for all is done in an hour. He scarce stays a minute; indeed, poor creature, he is a ghost, and cannot possibly last three months. The Dauphiness is in her bedchamber, but dressed and standing; looks cross, is not civil, and has the true Westphalian grace and accents. The four Mesdames, who are clumsy plump old wenches, with a bad likeness to their father, stand in a bedchamber in a row, with black cloaks and knotting-bags, looking good-humoured, not knowing what to say, and wriggling as if they wanted to make water. This ceremony too is very short.'

The Mozarts seemed to have fared better. They were escorted by the Swiss Guards to where the King and Queen were dining. King Louis sat with Queen Maria Leszczyńska on his left, while the Mozarts, in line with protocol, stood behind them, Wolferl between the King and the Queen, Leopold next to the Queen, and Nannerl and her mother beside the King.

'My Herr Wolfgangus stood all the time by the Queen,' wrote Leopold. 'talking continually to her, entertaining her and often kissing her hands and eating food she handed him from the table.' The Queen even interpreted the Mozarts' German for the King.

The Antichambre du Grand Couvert de la Reine, where the Mozarts were received, is one of the features of the palace of Versailles. There is, however, no proof that they played to the King and Queen, although the 'Avant-Coureur' of Paris ran a report dated March 5th 1764 that:

> 'these children had the honour of playing on several days to Mgr. the Dauphin, Mme the Dauphine, the Mesdames of France as well as to a great many persons of distinction from both court and town. The young Mozart also had the honour to play the organ in the King's Chapel at Versailles for an hour and a half in the presence of this eminent company.'

A week later, on January 8th 1764, the Mozarts returned to Paris, having been handsomely rewarded by King Louis XV, to the tune of fifty louis d'or.

SCENE TWO

Wolferl's First Published Works

Leopold Mozart did not like Paris. 'You would like perhaps to know how I like Paris?' he wrote. 'If I were to give you all the details neither the hide of a cow or of a rhinoceros would be enough.'

He was scathing about many aspects of Parisian life and tastes. He wrote very disparagingly of their habit of sending new-born babies to the countryside to be reared, where 'they fall in fires, or have their hands eaten away by pigs.'

On the countless beggars in the filthy streets, he maintains that: 'You have only to . . . walk through a couple of streets to find some blind or lame or hobbling or half-decomposing beggar.'

On the subject of music, he asserts that 'the whole of French music is worthless.'

Leopold was generalizing. The musical scenario of Paris in 1763 was a little more complex than that.

One of the leading musical figures in Paris was the eighty year old Jean Philippe Rameau. He was born in Dijon in 1683, and settled in Paris after spending many years in Italy, Avignon, Clermont and Lyon, where he held a variety of posts, including those of actor, organist and harpiscord teacher. He also wrote extensive treatises on harmony, acoustics and the science of music. These works, along with Jean-Jacques Rousseau's *Encyclopaedia of Music*, later became the definitive musical reference books well into the nineteenth century. He went to Paris in 1726 to publish his treatises, and enjoyed his first real success as a composer in 1733 with *Hippolyte et Aricie*. After that he turned out operas and ballets in abundance, and was officially recognized by Louis XV, who gave him a court appointment and a pension in recognition of his contribution to French music.

Rameau died the same year that the Mozarts left Paris; whether or not he heard Wolfgang performing, or whether he had even heard of him, is not recorded.

In the meantime, Paris was in the throes of a trend war between the Italian and French factions. This was in effect a living debate, in which such issues as classical art, mercilessly topical opera buffa, nature and enlightened radicalism were played out on both theatrical and world stages simultaneously. The debate was eventually to grow into the infamous Gluck-Piccini factionalism that almost gave rise to a form of early 'opera hooliganism.'

Leopold whose bias was definitely German, if anything, was very pleased to report that German music was emerging as a third force, and one to be reckoned with.

'The German composers are the leaders in publishing their compositions,' he wrote, perhaps too optimistically. He lists the harpsicordist Johann Schobert (1735–67), composer of sonatas for clavier and violin. These greatly influenced Wolferl, who wrote a number of similar sonatas during the Grand Tour, most of them dedicated to ladies of rank.

Another of Wolferl's influences was Johann Gottfried Eckhardt, Schobert's rival in almost every respect, as were Honnauer (1717–1809), Le Grand, the organist at St Germain des Prés and the harpist Christian Hochbrucker. They all brought their engraved sonatas to present to Wolferl and Nannerl, who gratefully accepted and performed them.

Only Schobert was far from pleased when Nannerl sight-read his sonatas. Leopold stated that, 'the vile Schobert cannot conceal his petty jealousy and is making a laughing stock of himself.'

It was no laughing matter, however, when three years later, Schobert gathered what he thought were some mushrooms in a wood near Paris and took them home to be cooked. As a result, Schobert, his cook, his family and three friends all died.

Be that as it may, Wolferl did not allow these petty crises to interfere with his creative processes, which were now beginning to take serious hold. He was critically appraising

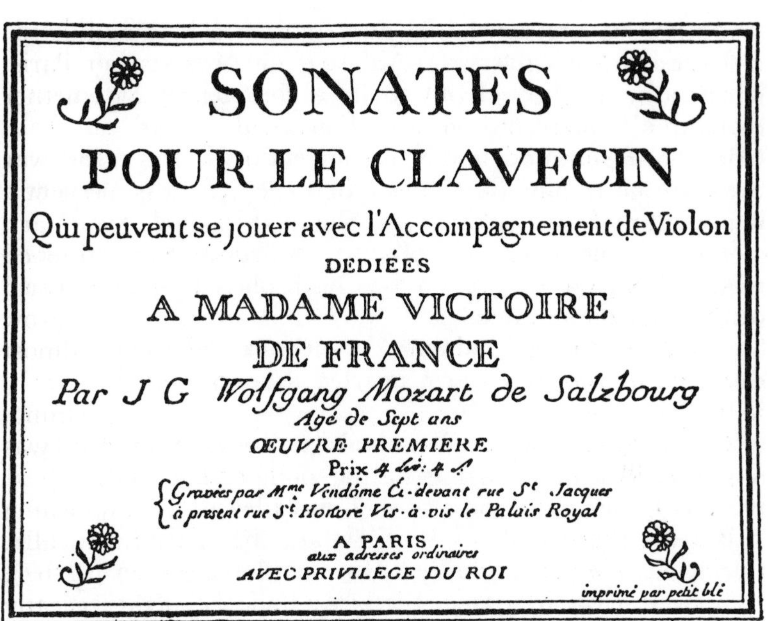

SONATES

POUR LE CLAVECIN

Qui peuvent se jouer avec l'Accompagnement de Violon

DEDIÉES

A MADAME VICTOIRE

DE FRANCE

Par J G Wolfgang Mozart de Salzbourg

Agé de Sept ans

OEUVRE PREMIERE

Prix 4 liv: 4 s

Gravées par M.me Vendôme Ci-devant rue St Jacques
à present rue St Honoré Vis-à-vis le Palais Royal

A PARIS
aux adresses ordinaires

AVEC PRIVILEGE DU ROI

imprimé par petit blé

The title page of Mozart's first published compositions.

Source: from an old print.

the music with which he had been coming into contact, while at the same time his compositions were maturing considerably. Gone were the days of his famous Minuet in F, and other childlike clavier pieces. He had been turning his attention to the clavier and violin sonata, especially those in the style of Schobert, in which the clavier was the dominant instrument, with the violin playing a supportive role.

A supportive role of a different kind was played at this time by the King's three remaining unmarried daughters, the 'Mesdames' Adelaide, Victoire and Sophie.

The King had five daughters all told. The first two, who were twins, were married, while the other three remained spinsters, and became permanent, if somewhat pathetic, fixtures at court.

Madame Adelaide, born in 1732, had been the King's

favourite. At first they had adored each other, and Louis forbade her from marrying. Although she was very pretty in her youth, she turned out to be a thoroughly unpleasant, bigoted old maid, whom the King called 'rag' or 'dish-cloth'. She was undeniably unconventional, and spent her maturity after the Revolution in exile, playing the jew's harp and making napkin rings. She died in 1800.

The Cabinet Doré de Madame Adelaide in Versailles, where Wolfgang was reputed to have played for her, is one of the palace's features.

A year younger, Madame Victoire was, like her mother, dull and plump, but warm hearted. She, too, died in exile, in 1799.

Finally, Madame Sophie, born the year after Madame Victoire, was ugly, had irritating mannerisms and walked with a strange gait. She also died in exile, in 1782.

But all three took to Wolferl, and he played for them during his stay in Versailles. He must have got on particularly well with Madame Victoire, since he dedicated the first two of his sonatas for clavier and violin to her: *K6 in C,* and *K7 in D.*

Two more sonatas were forthcoming to the Countess Adrienne Catherine de Tessé, who had been a lady-in-waiting to the Dauphine. She was the sister of Maréchal de Noailles, who was to be responsible, in 1770, in officially welcoming to France Wolferl's little friend and sometime 'fiancée' from a year previously: Princess Marie Antoinette, daughter of Emperor Francis I and Empress Maria Theresia of Austria, come to take her fateful place as the wife of the future King Louis XVI.

At this time, the Maréchal's sister kept a salon, and was famous for her charm and wit. Wolfgang played for her in her salon at Versailles, and she rewarded him with a gold snuff-box as a sign of her enchantment. Wolferl reciprocated by dedicating the Sonatas *K8 in B flat* and *K9 in G* to her.

And all the while, Wolferl was not only conquering Paris, but also furthering the cause of German music.

But his euphoria left him abruptly. Countess van Eyck had been confined indoors, suffering from a cold. On Sunday 28th January, she got up, went to church, and on her return sat chatting to Wolferl before lunch.

'She talked a great deal to Wolfgang as usual,' wrote Leopold. 'On Monday night I heard a carriage come into the courtyard and then some noises in the house. In the morning I heard that the Countess was ill and had coughed up a lot of blood. She is now unconscious and it is unlikely that she will recover and we shall never see her again. My children weep and pray . . .'

Countess van Eyck died of consumption on February 6th. Needless to say, the Mozarts were devastated. 'The sun cannot always shine,' wrote Leopold, 'and clouds often gather . . .'

Wolferl was inconsolable, and cried his eyes out.

SCENE THREE

Red Tape

After the death of Countess van Eyck, on March 4th, the Mozarts moved out of the Hotel Beauvais. Wolferl himself became ill and, 'in the night had such an inflammation of the throat that he was in danger of suffocating.'

Leopold took stock of the family's sojourn in Paris so far. His children were very successful in the salons of the capital. The general feeling was summed up in an article that appeared in the *Avant Coureur* dated March 5th, 1764:

> 'M. Mozart, musical director to his highness the Prince Archbishop of Salzburg, has been in the capital for several months with his two marvellous children. His daughter, aged eleven, plays the clavier in such a way that a more precise and brilliant execution would be hard to find. His son, who is just seven years old, is a real prodigy. He has all the talent and assurance of a maitre de chapelle. Not only does he perform the works of the most celebrated composers in Europe in an astonishing way, but he also composes himself. He extemporizes for hours on end, and, drawing on the inspiration of his genius, he blends the most exquisite ideas with the richest of harmonies. Those who understand what music is will in the end be amazed that in this child lie qualities that they would admire in the most accomplished maitre de chapelle. One can put this astonishing child through all the tests. Give him a theme without a bass, or ask him to write in a ground bass, and he will do it without recourse to either a

> clavier or a violin, without which few composers can write. Give him a violin part, and he will play it on the clavier putting in the necessary bass. Often he will also put in the middle voices. He will accompany by ear any melody sung to him, and even add any number of variations instantly. He has such a habitual command of the clavier that if one were to spread a cloth over the keyboard, it would still not prevent him from playing with the same precision and speed.'

They had achieved their primary objective, and played at the French court; and M. d'Hébert, Trésorier des Menus Plaisirs du Roi, had presented a gold snuff box from the King to Wolfgang inside which were fifty louis d'or.

On March 3rd Leopold lost the services of Sebastian Winter. The servant had secured another post with Prince von Fürstenberg, and left by country coach for Donaueschingen, in Württemberg, by way of Strasbourg. It was a double blow for the Mozarts, since not only had Leopold lost a good and efficient retainer, but Wolferl had lost a good friend, and esteemed fellow citizen of Rücken.

Leopold consequently engaged one Jean-Pierre Potivin as his friseur and servant to replace Sebastian Winter.

In the meantime, the family had had its portrait painted in water colours by Louis de Carmontelle (1716-1806), a protégé of the Duke of Orléans, and a friend of Grimm's.

'Wolfgang plays the clavier,' described Leopold, 'I stand behind his chair playing the violin, Nannerl leans on the clavier with one arm and with the other hand she holds music, as if she were singing.'

Leopold writes that M. de Carmontelle has painted the picture excellently well, although the artist had painted at least two pictures, one with Wolferl looking tiny, with his feet dantling just over the edge of his chair, while in the other, he looks a little older, more self-assured – and his feet touch the pedals.

Leopold had both engraved by the Basle-born copper engraver Christian von Mechel (1737–1817), who lived at the crossroads of the rue St Honoré and the rue de l'Echelle. Leopold chose the version of Wolferl looking tiny to make printed copies for general distribution among his friends. One can only speculate as to which of the two versions of young Wolferl was the more realistic, although something in between would be the most likely.

All the same, one can hardly blame Leopold for trying to make Wolfgang look younger than he really was. After all, he lied about the childrens' ages shamelessly throughout the whole of the Grand Tour!

Nevertheless, history and tradition have chosen the Carmontelle-Mechel print in which Wolfgang looks smaller as the definitive picture of the Mozarts as a musical family.

In the meantime, Wolferl recovered from his bout of fever, and resumed amazing Paris society with his ever-growing musicianship and technical prowess. Leopold wrote that Wolfgang: 'often accompanies soloists at public concerts. He transposes at first sight even when accompanying,' and boasted that Wolfgang could read Italian and German works 'a prima vista'.

What Leopold meant by public concerts in this instance is not certain, since there were no concerts in Paris at the time, apart from one.

The Concert Spirituel was an institution which marked the start of public concerts in France in 1725. Paris Opéra and the Theatre were protected, and no other music was allowed to compete, so these concerts were originally mounted only during Lent and Easter, when Opéra was suspended. They were held in the Great Hall in the Louvre called Cent Suisse, and were tightly organized so as not to encroach in any way on the Opéra's monopoly. The Cent Suisse was destroyed in the nineteenth century, and was situated where the Tuileries Gardens are today.

These concerts might be described as an eighteenth century version of the 'Proms', except that all competition was ruthlessly excluded.

However, it was possible to mount a public concert by cutting through red tape and obtaining permission. Leopold succeeded – but it was no easy feat:

'M. Grimm has managed everything for us,' he wrote.

This was not strictly speaking true, although Leopold may be forgiven for having bestowed on his primary benefactor more than was his due. Leopold wrote:

> 'He brought the business to court, took care of the first concert and he alone has paid me on his own account eighty louis d'or for 320 tickets. And he paid for the candles as more than sixty large wax ones were burnt. Grimm obtained the permits for the first concert and is taking care of the second, for which 100 tickets are already sold.'

The first concert took place on March 10th, in the 'theatre of M. Félix, in the rue et Porte St Honoré.'

Leopold described M. Félix as a 'distinguished gentleman' who had a small theatre in his house, 'where the nobles often acted and produced plays among themselves. I got this room through Mme de Clermont, who lives in the house.'

M. Félix and Mme de Clermont had houses opposite one another. The Porte St Honoré used to stand where the Rue Royale and the Rue St Honoré meet: and Mme Clermont's house was on the corner of the Rue St Honoré and the Rue St Florentin, which used to be called the Nouvelle Rue de l'Orangerie. The house stretched down this road almost as far as the Rue Rivoli, off the Place de la Concorde. This is only the site, since the actual house is no longer there.

M. Félix lived opposite, on the corner of Rue St Honoré and the Rue Richepanse, and the back of his house gave onto what is today the Place de la Madeleine. Once again, this is only the site.

However, it is evident that these two houses were spacious enough to accomodate concerts and theatrical productions. Which of the two houses served as the venue for the Mozarts' concerts is not clear, and Leopold's letter suggests that Mme de Clermont lived in M. Félix's house. Either Leopold was misinformed, or else Mme Clermont chose to live at M. Félix's, instead of the marital home for reasons not passed down in history.

The most likely venue was the house of M. Félix, who was known as a lover of the Arts and the Theatre; while Mme de Clermont most probably spent a lot of time at his house, involving herself with his thespian activities, and may well have given Leopold the impression that she lived there.

Leopold goes on to describe the bureaucracy involved in

staging an unofficial public concert in Paris; at the same time putting the record straight as to how many people, other than M. Grimm, were involved in the process:

> The permission to hold the two concerts was quite exceptional and is contrary to the privilege given by the King to the Opéra, the Concert Spirituel, and the French and Italian Theatres; and this permission was obtained from M. de Sartine, Lieutenant General of the Police, by the Duc de Chartres, the Duc de Duras, the Comte de Tessé, and many of the leading ladies who wrote to him.'

M. de Sartine agreed, and admission was strictly by ticket only. Leopold distributed these to his friends, who, in turn, peddled them around Paris. The majority of the tickets were in blocks of 12 or 24, and were given to ladies, 'who sell them easily,' Leopold pointed out wrily, 'because out of politeness no-one can refuse to buy.'

The concert was a great success, and Leopold took 112 louis d'or, so a second concert was arranged, at the same venue, on April 9th.

'Those two concerts brought us in so much money,' wrote Leopold with satisfaction.

Among many 'presents', Wolfgang was also given a miniature gold watch by the Comtesse de Tessé. When Vincent and Mary Novello visited Constanza Mozart in Salzburg in 1829, they noted that she was wearing it at the time.

The day after the second concert, the Mozarts left Paris for Calais in their own coach, with seven horses. Leopold had with him not only his new servant, Jean-Pierre Potivin, but had also engaged an Italian called Porta, who had been recommended as a servant, since he had done the journey eight times to date.

The old post road passed through the Porte de Clignancourt. It now follows the N14 through St Denis, then becomes for a very brief spell the D 916 to Breteuil, where it once more meets the N1, and continues all the way to Calais by way of Amiens, Abbeville, Montreuil and Boulogne.

Horace Walpole, on his way to Paris, was impressed with this route:

> 'I find this country wonderfully enriched since I saw it four and twenty years ago. Boulogne is grown quite a plump snug town, with a number of new houses. In truth, I impute this air of opulence a little to ourselves. The crumbs that fall from the chaises of the swarms of English that visit Paris, must have contributed to fatten this province.'

When they reached Calais the Mozarts stayed at the Hotel d'Angleterre, although they dined with the Procureur du Roi et de l'Amirauté, in whose care they left the coach prior to embarking on the boat to Dover.

Thomas Pennant was in Calais in 1765. 'The entrance into the harbour is bounded on each side by a bank faced with thick boards and defended by two forts built on piles,' he wrote. 'The harbour is small and incapable of receiving large vessels. The streets of Calais are straight but ill built. The market place is large; in it is the town house adorned with a high tower which is oddly terminated by a large crown of stone work. Near it is a polygonal tower to observe what ships pass and is called le Guet. The church is large; the great altar is composed of marble pillars and has in the middle a good piece by Rubens.'

The process of arranging the crossing was organized by the knowledgeable Porta, who came into his own with some hard work on the waterfront. The result was that Leopold eschewed the packet boat in favour of hiring a boat privately for five louis d'or, then selling tickets to four passengers at half a louis each. The crossing, therefore, cost him three louis, which was cheaper than the packet boat.

'What a good thing I employed him,' wrote Leopold, 'he arranged everything and did all the bargaining.'

ACT

3

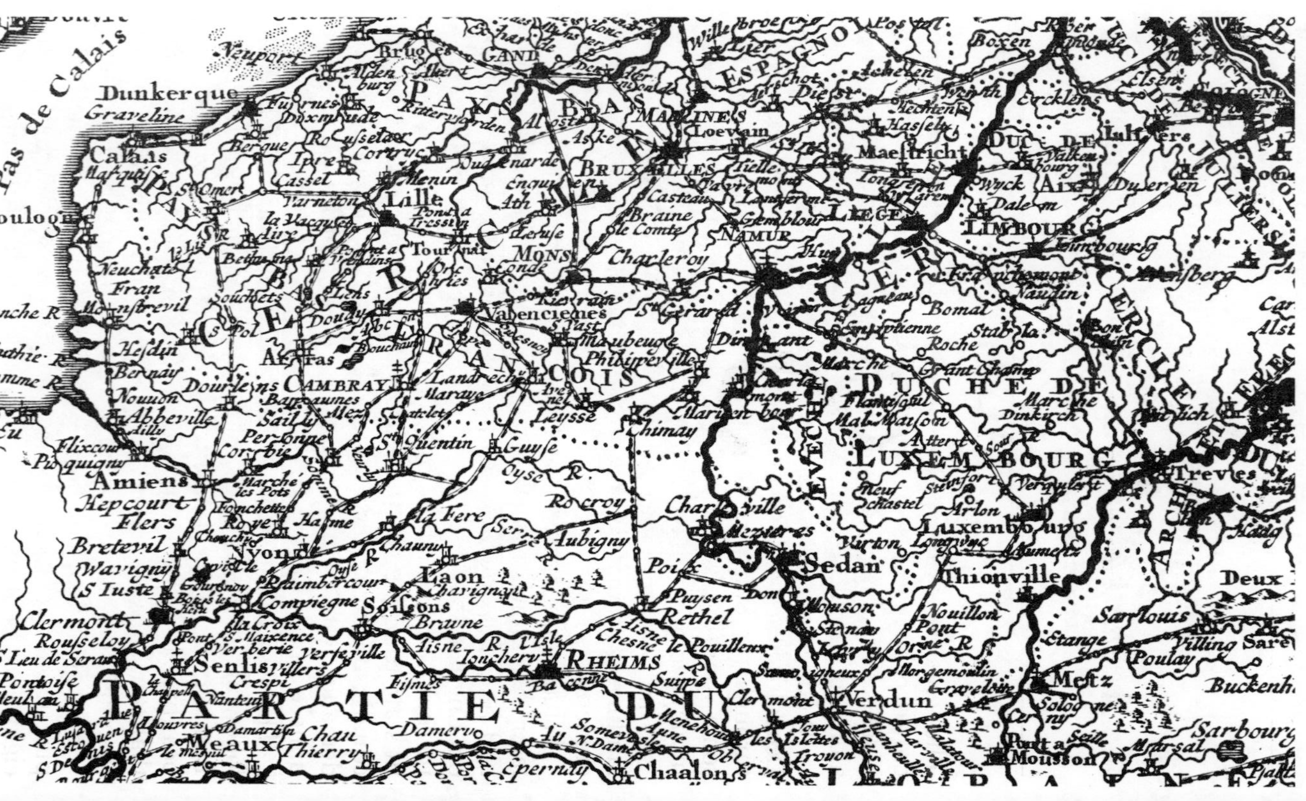

Pas de Calais
Dunkerque
Graveline
Calais
Neuport
Bruges
GAND
Lille
Tournai
MONS
Valenciennes
CAMBRAY
Arras
Amiens
Abbeville
BRUXELLES
MALINES
Loevain
NAMUR
Charleroy
Maestricht
LIEGE
LIMBOURG
DUCHE DE
LUXEMBOURG
Luxembourg
Treves
Thionville
Sedan
Rethel
RHEIMS
Laon
Soissons
Compiegne
Senlis
Clermont
Verdun
Metz
Chaalons
Meaux
PARTIE DU

PRELUDE AND SCENE ONE

At the Court of the King of England

The crossing was rough, and the tossing, pitching and crowded boat was accompanied by what Leopold took to be a school of porpoises, which rose and dived as they swam alongside the hull.

'We have, thank God, crossed the Maxglanerbach,' wrote Leopold, referring ironically to a little stream that flows through the Salzburg suburb of Maxglan. 'But not without some vomiting, and I was worst. It was a saving however of money we might have had to spend on emetics.'

What was more, in Dover they had to transfer to a smaller landing-craft to take them off the ship – at a cost of six gulden.

Whatever money may have been saved on emetics was later discharged to hordes of 'most obedient servants', who had beset the Mozarts at the very moment that they set foot on English soil, bent on carrying the Mozarts' luggage to the inn, and demanding payment. Since Leopold was in no fit state to argue that he already had two perfectly good and equally obedient servants of his own, he acceded to their demands, and only afterwards complained of the extra, unnecessary cost.

The Mozarts took a night's lodgings at an inn, and the following morning took the stage coach from Dover to London, by way of Canterbury. Leopold wrote that: 'the beautiful English horses with which we travelled ran so fast that the drivers could scarcely breathe because of the rushing wind. To us all this was both strange and pleasant.'

English roads had been notoriously bad until the Turnpike trusts were established during the second half of the eighteenth century. These trusts took it upon themselves to improve and maintain roads, in return for permission to charge tolls; the result was that travel became faster and infinitely more efficient. A Lord Chancellor of the second half of the eighteenth century, commented that: 'this speed was thought to be highly dangerous to the head, independently of all the perils of an overturn, and stories were told of men and women who having reached London with such celerity died suddenly of an affectation of the brain.'

The Mozarts' coach, however, survived these dangers, and Leopold was full of admiration for the English livestock that he saw grazing the greening Kent countryside. 'One sees in the fields the finest cattle and the lambs are as big as calves with wool that is thick and long,' he wrote.

The Mozarts reached London on April 23rd, after nearly a fortnight on post road and high sea, and put up at the White Bear in Piccadilly.

The White Bear was one of London's main coaching inns, a large building standing athwart an elongated courtyard where the coaches used to drive in. The building is no longer there, but the courtyard is now Eagle Place, a pedestrian street at the eastern end of Piccadilly; the inn itself was sited where the buildings in Eagle Place now stand.

The Mozarts also enjoyed an early taste of English cuisine, and Leopold found it very good. 'The food is extremely nourishing, substantial and strengthening,' he wrote. 'The beef, veal and lamb is better and finer than one can find in the whole world.'

He also commented on English drinks, to which his reactions were mixed. 'The beer is extraordinarily strong and good. On the other hand their wine is very sour and extremely acid. The coffee, for which one pays four gulden a pound, has to be roasted and ground, and there is a special shop for that. The tea kettle is on the fire all day long, and on visits one is served tea and bread and butter, that is, finely cut bread spread with butter. The midday meal is usually between two and three o'clock, and most people only eat some cheese, bread and butter at night.'

The Mozarts stayed at the White Bear for one night, after which they moved into lodgings at the house of Mr Cousin, a hair cutter (Leopold writes: Mr Couzin, a 'hare cutter') in Cecil Court, St Martin's Lane. This is a short pedestrian street off St Martin's Lane adjacent to Leicester Square Underground station, today a treasure trove full of specialist second-hand bookshops, print shops and record shops. Cecil Court has been completely rebuilt, but the site of Mr Cousin's house is traditionally recognized as where Nos 19–21 now stand.

On April 27th, the Mozarts gave their first performance in London, at the Court of the King of England. The venue was in the Queen's Palace in St James' Park – which is now Buckingham Palace, the London residence of the Royal Family.

King George III was also the Elector of Hanover. He was born in 1738, and succeeded his grandfather, George II, to the throne in 1760. The following year, he married Sophia Charlotte von Mecklenburg-Strelitz. Both the twenty-seven year old king and his twenty-one year old queen were ardent music lovers, as were the first two Hanoverian kings. It was George I who, while still at his Electoral court in Hanover, had first employed Handel, who was even now the present King's favourite composer. Queen Charlotte was also a musician, who played the clavier and sang.

The concert was a great success, and, 'the graciousness with which His Majesty the King and Her Majesty the Queen received us is indescribable,' gushed Leopold, adding that their easy manner and friendly ways made the Mozarts forget that these were the King and Queen of England.

Wolfgang went on to impress the court by sightreading various compositions that the King had placed before him. There were works by two German composers who had chosen to live and work in London, Carl Friedrich Abel (1723–87) and Johann Christian Bach. Wolferl was particularly struck by the latter's music – with significant results in the months to come. There were items by Georg Christoph Wagenseil, court composer to the Empress Maria Theresia of Austria, which no doubt reminded Wolferl of the time he played at another, equally royal court, when he received a famous kiss of recognition.

He then accompanied Queen Charlotte in an aria which she sang.

However, no concert at the English court at this time would be complete without something by the grand old man of English music – that sophisticated German sybarite and charming *bon viveur* whose prolific output had enchanted London – on and off – for so many years – George Frederick Handel.

Handel was born in Halle, Saxony, in 1685, the same year as Johann Sebastian Bach, the father of Johann Christian. Having gained his earliest musical experiences as organist at Halle Cathedral, violinist and keyboard player at the Hamburg opera orchestra as well as four years in Italy experimenting with Italian opera, he secured a post at the court of Georg Ludwig, the Elector of Hanover in 1710. During this appointment, Handel took frequent leaves of absence, often indefinite. This displeased the Elector, and a great deal of bad feeling developed between them.

Handel's absences frequently took him to London, a city that he grew to love, and ultimately chose as his permanent home. However, he omitted to let the Elector know of his plans, which was a mistake since, on the death of Queen Anne in 1714, his former employer inherited the throne of England as King George I.

This proved to be embarrassing, since Handel had already been in the employment of the Earl of Buckingham, where he had been making a name for himself as a virtuoso and a composer, since the previous year. An apocryphal story relates that he wrote the *Water Music* for performance on royal river trips on the Thames, as an apology and a peace offering to the new king. The work was graciously accepted in the spirit in which it was intended, and the way was smoothed for Handel to go on to become the most famous 'English' composer, unencumbered by royal displeasure.

He progressed to an appointment with the Duke of Chandos, before taking up opera promotion at the King's Theatre, Haymarket, which gave him the chance to compose numerous operas, mostly in the Italian style. He became enormously popular, and this popularity gave him enough freedom to develop the English Oratorio, with such masterpieces as *Saul*, *Israel in Egypt* and, the most celebrated of them all, the *Messiah*. This Oratorio so delighted King George II that he stood up during the *Hallelujah Chorus*, a gesture that is traditionally emulated by audiences to this day.

For forty years Handel's lot had fluctuated from fame and fortune to decline and debt, according to changing vogues, style wars and factionalism – an occupational hazard for all composers.

Wolfgang may or may not have been aware that Handel had died only five years previously, aged seventy-four and blind, much lamented by the royal family as well as the London music scene. So it was no surprise that there should have been some of Handel's works lying there, among the rest of the music. Wolferl picked these up, took the bass part of an air, and played the most beautiful melody on it.

'Everyone,' wrote Leopold, 'was amazed.'

Only one thing slightly marred the occasion as far as the financially astute Leopold was concerned. The recital did not bring in as much money as he had hoped.

'Only 24 guineas,' scrawled Leopold. In the course of doing his accounts, Leopold had worked out that a guinea was equivalent to a louis d'or.

SCENE TWO

When in Rome . . .

Leopold had certain reservations about the English capital.

'Now it appears to me that in London everyone is in fancy dress,' he wrote, 'and my wife and my little girl both wear English hats, while I and our big Wolfgang are dressed in English suits.'

Whatever Leopold thought of English fashions, Nannerl and her mother were absolutely delighted with them – especially since they were both very fashion-conscious. Even in later years, when Maria Anna accompanied her son on his second journey to Paris in 1778, she always made a point of writing to Nannerl, letting her know what was being worn in Munich, Mannheim and Paris that year. Nannerl appreciated these regular updates to trends. In fact, Nannerl had taken the opportunity to wear the English hat that she had received as a 'present' in Mainz.

But when in Rome, Leopold realized, one must do as the Romans do, so he kitted his family out *à l'anglaise*. A week after their appearance at Court, they were desporting themselves in St James' Park thus attired, when the King and Queen drove past.

> 'Although we were wearing other clothes, they recognized us and not only greeted us, but the King opened his window, leaned out and nodded his head and greeted us and especially our Master Wolfgang.'

One wonders whether Leopold desported himself thus on purpose, in the hope of being seen. A similar coincidence in Munich the previous year had resulted in the family

Roche Map of London.

Source: from an old print.

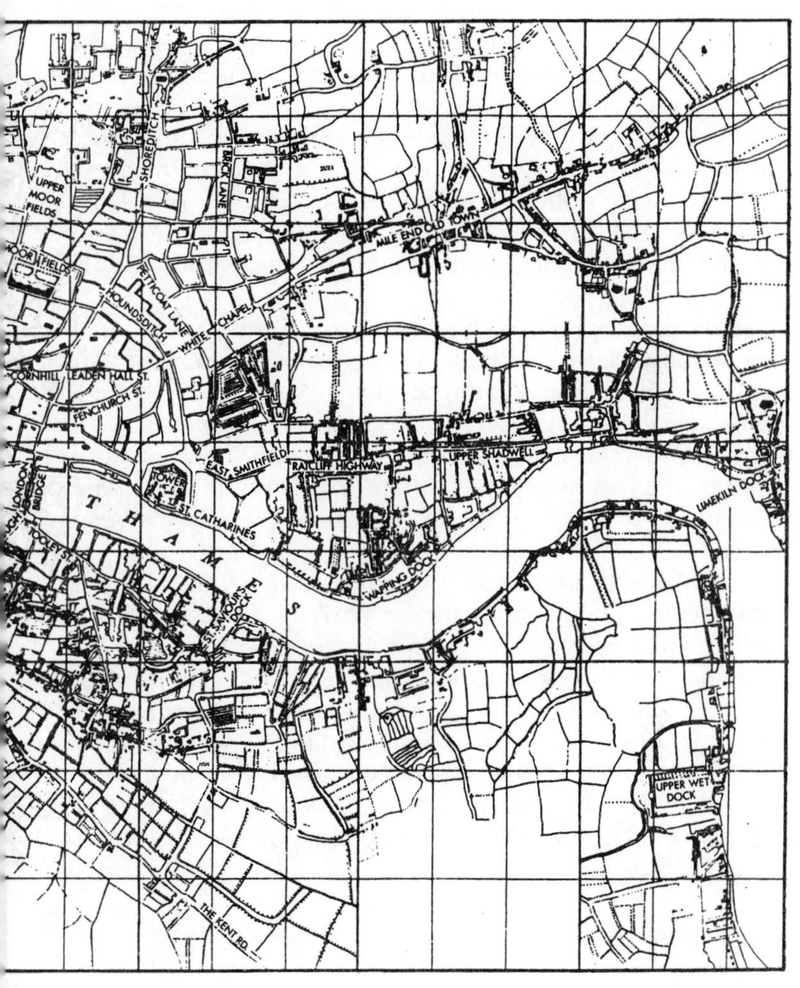
UPPER MOOR FIELDS
MOOR FIELDS
SHOREDITCH
BRICK LANE
MILE END OLD TOWN
PETTICOAT LANE
HOUNDSDITCH
WHITE CHAPEL
CORNHILL
LEADEN HALL ST.
FENCHURCH ST.
EAST SMITHFIELD
RATCLIFF HIGHWAY
UPPER SHADWELL
LIMEKILN DOCK
LONDON BRIDGE
TOWER
ST. CATHARINES
T H A M E S
TOOLEY ST.
ST. SAVIOUR'S DOCK
WAPPING DOCK
UPPER WET DOCK
THE KENT RD.

entertaining the Electoral court in Munich the same evening, when the family showed themselves in the grounds of the Nymphenburg Palace. On this occasion, the Mozarts did not perform for the English Court that same evening, but the occurrence may well have contributed to another intimate recital at Court.

'We were again with the King and Queen on the evening of the 19th May from 6 to 10 in the evening,' wrote Leopold, 'with nobody else present except the two Princes, (probably the Dukes of York and Gloucester) who are the King's brothers, and another, the brother of the Queen.'

Apart from playing the clavier and the violin, Wolferl also displayed his skill at the organ - which particularly impressed the King. Nannerl, in her later recollections - in which she curiously refers to Leopold and Wolfgang as 'the father' and 'the son' respectively, mentions that at this concert 'the son also played the King's organ, and everyone thought his organ playing far superior to his clavier playing.'

The Mozarts played to the royal family on a third and final occasion much later in the year, on October 25th, the fourth anniversary of the King's accession.

Leopold had arranged for the childrens' public London debut at a concert at Hickford's in Brewer Street on May 17th. Unable to find accompanying musicians, their appearance had to be postponed until the next concert scheduled for May 22nd, but once more, they had to drop out, since this time Wolferl had caught a cold. Leopold wrote:

> 'I must explain to you that in England there is a sort of native illness which they call 'a cold' which is why you almost never see people in summer clothes, they all wear cloth garments. This so-called cold is for people who are not constitutionally sound, so dangerous, that many develop 'consumption' as they call it here; and for such people the best course is to leave England and go overseas, where there are many examples of people getting better.'

Fortunately, the drastic action that Leopold had described as a cure was not necessary, and Wolferl soon recovered without recourse to a trip abroad. A benefit concert, or 'concerto al nostro profitto,' as Leopold called it, was finally arranged for June 5th, at noon, in the magnificent Great Room, Spring Garden.

This was the venue where that very year Johann Christian Bach and Carl Friedrich Abel had established a series of regular public concerts, so it is more than likely that Johann Christian had set up the venue for the Mozarts.

A contemporary exhibition catalogue describes this all-purpose venue as:

> 'fitted up in an elegant manner: on the ceiling of the dome are fine paintings in chiaro oscuro, by a celebrated artist, as are the sides of the dome by the same . . . In the centre of the room, and at each end, are five magnificent crystal lustres, finely cut; four lesser lustres are also suspended from the mouths of the dragons at the corners of the dome: other chandeliers and girandoles of crystal are also placed, wherever light is necessary to be transmitted; curtains of crimson are let down by machines to cover the pieces, which are also enclosed in a balustrade of white and gold: the doors are also white and gold, finely ornamented. A carpet covers the whole room, also the stairs; and by a very curious contrivance, warm air is introduced into the room at pleasure.'

There is no doubt that Leopold thoroughly approved of the venue.

The postponement was probably not such a bad thing, since the rich and influential were mostly out of town during May anyway, returning only in time for the King's birthday celebrations on June 4th, which was a public holiday. This year, the Duke of Northumberland had arranged a fête, with 10,000 lamps and fireworks, in the grounds of the Queen's Palace for 1,500 guests. With these festivities as well as the inevitable social rounds, Leopold was worried that no one would come to a benefit concert, particularly as it was not the concert season anyway. Still, he decided to go ahead regardless, since it would have been an opportunity wasted, especially in such a splendid venue.

'We must take the risk,' he wrote, 'and profit by this opportunity to become known.'

The London Gazette subsequently carried the announcement:

> 'At the Great Room in Spring Gardens, near St James' Park, Tuesday, June 5th, will be performed a grand concert of
>
> Vocal and Instrumental Music
>
> For the benefit of Miss MOZART of eleven, and Master MOZART, of seven years of age, Prodigies of Nature; taking the opportunity of representing to the Public the greatest Prodigy that Europe or that Human Nature has to boast of. Every Body will be astonished to hear a Child of such a tender Age playing the Harpsicord in such Perfection. It surmounts all Fantastic and Imagination, and it is hard to express which is more astonishing, his Execution upon the Harpsicord at Sight, or his own Composition. His Father brought him to England, not doubting that he will meet with Success in a Kingdom, where his Countryman, that late famous Vertuoso Handel, received during his Life-time such particular Protection. Tickets at Half a Guinea each; to be had of Mr Mozart, at Mr Couzin's, Hair-Cutter; in Cecil Court, St Martin's Lane.'

Leopold need not have worried about lack of attendance, for he sold over two hundred tickets to 'all the leading people in London'. This was quite a good turnout considering it was summer. It is true, that during the winter months, he may well have filled the Great Room up with six hundred, but this time he was not complaining.

'I have again had a shock,' he wrote, 'namely taking in one hundred guineas in three hours!'

His shock, however, was modified when he had to pay all the expenses: hire of hall, five guineas, two claviers (there was an unidentified concerto for two claviers in the programme), half a guinea each; musicians between half a guinea to five guineas each, according to their importance.

In fact the expenses came to only twenty guineas, since many of the musicians, obviously influenced by the talent of the two children, waived their fees and gave their services for free.

Leopold summed the concert up by recording that 'everyone was delighted.'

Although new buildings were erected on the site of the Great Room in 1825, Spring Gardens is still there, a short crescent round the Admiralty Arch at the top of The Mall, facing Trafalgar Square. The Great Room was where the British Council building now stands.

On June 29th, Leopold allowed Wolferl to play at a concert to help raise money for the Lying-in Hospital that was to be built near Westminster Bridge. The venue was the Rotunda in Ranelagh Gardens, situated on the embankment of the River Thames at Chelsea, off the Chelsea Bridge Road. The Rotunda was a circular pavilion with a stage and an organ, where concerts, exhibitions and various events were mounted. Ranelagh Gardens is still there, by the north end of Chelsea Bridge, although the Rotunda has been demolished.

'I shall let Wolfgang play a concerto on the organ at this concert,' wrote Leopold trying to sound condescending, 'and through this act become an English patriot. You see, this is the way to win the affection of this very special nation.'

One finds it a little difficult to ascertain just what Leopold thought of the English; at one moment they were a 'very special nation', while in the next, he writes that 'the majority of the inhabitants have no religion and where I have only evil examples before me.'

SCENE THREE

The Guru and the Acolyte

One of the most important figures who featured in the early Mozart story was Johann Christian Bach. He was born in Leipzig in 1735, the youngest surviving son of Johann Sebastian Bach. He was trained by his elder half-brother, Carl Philip Emanuel, after which he spent a long time in Italy before coming to live and work in London, in 1763. Like Handel before him, he wrote and produced Italian operas. He then teamed up with Carl Abel to arrange regular concerts at Carlyle House – an institution that ran successfully for seventeen years. He was also music master to Queen Charlotte, and it was in this capacity that he would have been present at the royal concerts.

Wolfgang and the older composer instantly took to one another - both personally and musically. Personally, Wolfgang saw in Johann Christian a very kind man, young, full of warmth and wit, who would tease, amuse and play with Wolfgang and treat him as a boy rather than a genius. He was obviously a man who had a way with children – for who else would stand Wolferl between his knees at the harpsicord while he sat behind him, and play duets with him, improvising together or separately, or just playing a bar each. It was pure musical sparring, like arm-wrestling – supposedly devoid of any real intellectual content, although intellectual content was surely present if only because of the stature of the contestants. Maybe Wolferl needed an uncle-figure with whom he could have fun and 'muck about' at the keyboard, without the encumbrance of his father's seriousness and idealism. Nor was he expected to perform conjuring tricks like playing while his hands were covered with cloth, or writing in bass lines to given melodies.

Wolferl greatly enjoyed meeting the composer at Court, or visiting him at his home in Meard Street, and later in Jermyn Street, where he could be just a little boy instead of a performing seal.

Johann Christian Bach must have been very good for Wolferl at this time, since the boy had been feeling homesick again, missing Salzburg and listing his absent friends.

On a musical level, the older man had a profound effect on Wolferl. Here was a composer and a musician who was obviously a cut above his own father: the boy's developing maturity of intellect and musicianship had begun to be much more discerning, and he was by now discriminating not only between the good and the mediocre, but also between one style and another. No longer were his father's models the definitive ones. He had already showed an interest in the creative processes of Schobert and Eckhardt in Paris – but now, his ears were being opened to two specific forms: the beautiful melodic invention of the Italian aria, and the tight structuralism of the 3-part Overture, a form which both composers had honed, nurtured and developed into a perfect musical structure: the Symphony.

Leopold knew little about opera, and the symphony belonged to a new generation of composers – among whom Johann Christian Bach was not only a leading light, but also undoubtedly the father of the classical symphony as we understand the term today, while Mozart was the acolyte who would go on to become the master.

His father was not able to do much for Wolferl as far as symphonies and operas were concerned, so Wolferl turned to emulate the man who could, and by 1765 he had assimilated enough of Bach's music to make a start. He was going to write an opera – for young people – and produce it when he got back to Salzburg. The opera never actually materialized – at least, not in London – but Wolferl did give the matter some serious thought during his London months; he did compose two arias, *'Va dal furor portata' K21*, written in London, and *'Conservati fidele' K23*, written later in the year in The Hague.

Set to texts by Metastasio, they constitute a starting point on a voyage that was to culminate so gloriously with *Don Giovanni* in 1787.

If the opera idea was pie-in-the-sky, the symphony was not, even though the circumstances were in many ways unfortunate.

It all began on the evening of July 8th, at the close of a glorious summer's day, when the Mozart children had an engagement to perform at Lord Thanet's house in Grosvenor Square. Unfortunately, carriages were hard to come by that evening, so Leopold settled for a sedan chair for the children, while he decided to walk 'as the weather was unusually fine.'

However, the bearers walked very fast, and Leopold almost had to jog to keep up – no mean feat for a portly, unfit, middle aged lover of the comforts of life! Especially all the way from Cecil Court to Grosvenor Square, just over a mile as the crow flies, but possibly nearer two as the sedan bearers walked. At Lord Thanet's he sweated profusely all evening, despite the slight night chill that wafted into the house throught the open windows. Returning home that night, he hired two sedans, since he was now feeling too ill to walk back to Cecil Court.

Despite trying to sweat it off, his condition deteriorated, and he became seriously ill, with a sore throat and increased fever. But help was at hand. An unnamed Portuguese Jewish doctor of his acquaintance dosed him with 'rhubarb powder', and 'that achieved a smooth evacuation,' bringing Leopold temporary relief.

Leopold tried to return the favour by converting the doctor to Catholicism. 'I took pains to bring the idea of our faith to him.'

He failed.

'Patience!' he wrote optimistically, 'I shall perhaps yet be a missionary in England.'

From a Catholic in staunchly Protestant eighteenth century England, those were fighting words indeed!

At the beginning of August he was still unwell, and on the 6th the family moved to Dr Randall's house in Chelsea, where they spent the next seven weeks. Leopold wrote:

> 'I find myself now in a spot outside the town, where they brought me in a sedan chair, so that through the good air I might get a better appetite

> and fresh strength. It is one of the finest views in the world. Wherever I look I see nothing but gardens and in the distance the finest palaces and where I am living the house itself has a lovely garden.'

Chelsea was, at the time, a village outside London, known for green and pleasant surroundings as well as its wholesome clean air.

Maria Anna had been doing all the cooking, since the food sent in from a local eating house was so awful. Wolferl was not allowed to play any instruments, and had to keep quiet while his father was unwell. So he spent a great deal of time with Nannerl and Dr Randall's children, playing in the garden; his known love of gardens may date from his stay in Chelsea.

When not playing outside, Wolferl amused himself by composing, and it was during this time that he first tried his hand at the Symphony, with Nannerl sitting quietly beside him, copying, drawing – and possibly writing up her travel diary, of which about a third is devoted to notes about London. It is likely that not being allowed to play any instruments may have contributed to Wolferl's symphonic thinking, disciplining himself into 'hearing' with his mind's ear without recourse to a clavier. This technique was to become a predominant factor in his composing process in the years to come, when he 'heard' and retained complete symphonies in his mind; writing them down was merely a question of copying out onto manuscript paper what was already there.

In later life, Nannerl recalled when he was writing his first Symphony: 'I used to sit by him as he was composing, and he said to me, "remind me to give the French horns plenty to do!"'

French horns were very popular in England at the time – Handel had often made excellent use of their strident, ringing tones, especially in music designed for outdoor performance. So whether or not Wolferl needed Nannerl's reminder was immaterial. Two horns, like twin heralds holding in trust the promise of his final jewels of the form, are kept prominent and busy in the second movement.

Fanfares accompanying the first giant steps to 'Jupiter'!

The house, in Five Fields Row, is still there, now at 180 Ebury Street, Chelsea, SW1. A plaque commemorates the composition of Mozart's First Symphony there.

Under the direct influence of his new found guru, Wolferl composed six symphonies, or symphonic fragments during 1764, of which *K16 in E flat (No.1)* and *K19 in D (No.4)* are complete, and frequently performed.

The relationship between Wolfgang and Johann Christian grew into a strong and lasting friendship as Wolferl grew up, and the two composers expressed a strong admiration for one another.

'I love him and respect him with all my heart,' wrote twenty-one year old Wolfgang in 1778. 'He has praised me warmly not only to my face, but to others also.'

When Johann Christian Bach died on New Year's Day in 1782, Mozart was heartbroken, especially as he recalled their halcyon London days, which saw the definitive germination of Mozart the Master of opera and of the symphony.

'What a loss to the musical world!' he wrote sadly.

SCENE FOUR

The Three Italians of Brewer Street

On September 25th, Leopold recovered, and took stock of the situation. Seven weeks of enforced idleness had taken its toll on the family finances. He had worked out that it would cost £300 a year to keep a family 'in strictest economy,' and they had spent 170 guineas since the beginning of July alone, so there was no time to waste: money had to be earned.

The first thing to do was to move back into London, in order to be in the thick of things, particularly as summer was over and the 'season' was beginning. So the Mozarts took lodgings with a Mr Thomas Williamson, a staymaker, at 20 Frith Street, in Soho (sometimes misspelt Thrift Street). The house is no longer there, but the site is where No 21 is today.

'Now come a few months when I have a lot to do to bring the Nobility on to my side,' he wrote. 'That will take lots of galloping around and trouble.'

So with renewed vigour, all thanks to seven weeks of rest, care and wholesome Chelsea air, Leopold set about building up more contacts and arranging for various private performances in the noble houses of London. As always, he jotted down the names of those he considered significant.

For this purpose, he used his very special notebook, in which he recorded just about everything worth recording – names, addresses, dates, events. He never went anywhere without his notebook. When he wrote his letters to Lorenz Hagenauer, he always referred to his notebook. Although today, Leopold's *Reiseaufzeichnungen* is an invaluable document and a trove of information, a great deal of it is meaningless to the modern reader, because of the amount of facts jotted down for Leopold's own reference, which are out of all context.

However, a glance at his London pages shows a number of aristocratic and diplomatic names, including the French and Danish ambassadors'. The owners of some of these names, given his erratic English spelling, can only be guessed at, and we can only speculate whether Wolferl gave private concerts in their houses, whether they constituted part of Leopold's social scene, or whether they were merely useful addresses.

A browse among the names can reveal some interesting insights into contemporary musical life, as in the case of the Three Italians of Brewer Street.

At the top of Leopold's list of names, after that of the King, are Mr Bach and Mr Abel. Apart from arranging their regular series of concerts at various venues in London, including the Great Room at Spring Gardens, Messrs Bach and Abel were also heavily involved with the Italian opera scene as originally established by Handel. A glance further down the pages of Leopold's notebook shows lists of names like 'Mr Mazziotti – musico soprano; Mr Giustinelli – musico soprano; and Mr Guglietti – l'ultimo Cantante un Basso; all these,' – Leopold's notes are often in Italian – 'I have found in Mazziotti's house – at a dinner in Brewer Street.'

Leopold was referring to the street where Hickford's Rooms were situated.

Hickford's Rooms were the best and most fashionable concert venue in London at the time, and a favourite stage for Italian musicians since the early eighteenth century. Mr Mazziotti had evidently taken a house in the same street.

Originally between Panton Street and James Street, it consisted of a large room rented for performing purposes from John Hickford, who ran a dancing school on the premises. It boasted such contemporary luminaries as Francesco Geminiani, Francesco Veracini, and Pietro Castrucci, who was a pupil of Corelli and went on to become the leader of Handel's opera orchestra.

So successful was the venue, that it moved to its own premises at 41 Brewer Street in 1738, whence it continued to flourish as Hickford's Concert Rooms, the venue of the finest Italian music to be heard in London at the time. The building was pulled down in 1936 to make room for the Regent Palace Hotel Annexe, and is today numbered as 65 Brewer Street, Soho.

Wolferl was extensively exposed to this Italian connection, for his interest and expertise in Italian opera and vocal music was considerable, even before the end of the year. Among these names the most significant as far as Wolferl was concerned were two castrati, Giustino Tenducci (1736–90) and Giovanni Manzuoli (1725–80).

Little is known of Tenducci's relationship with Wolferl at this time, except that they originally met through J C Bach. Wolferl liked him very much, enjoyed his singing, and learnt a great deal about opera from him. Tenducci became very fond of Wolferl, and in 1778 they met again in Paris as adults and good friends.

An extract from Smollett's *Humphry Clinker* 1771 – says:

> 'At Ranelagh I heard the famous Tenducci, a thing from Italy: it looks for all the world like a man, though they say it is not. The voice to be sure is neither man's nor woman's but it is more melodious than either, and it warbled so divinely that while I listened I really thought myself in paradise.'

Manzuoli played a more important part in Wolferl's development. A singer of enormous popularity with a large following, Manzuoli was the most important vocalist in the 'Bach-Abel stable'. Aware of the boy's growing interest in Italian opera, he gave Wolferl singing lessons – not so much to teach him to sing – Wolferl had a tuneful voice – but to teach him those singing techniques that would help him in writing for the voice.

Horace Walpole, in his letter of November 25th 1764, wrote:

> 'I went to town to hear Manzuoli, who did not quite answer my expectation, though a very fine singer, but his voice has been younger, and wants the touching tones of Elisi. However, the

> audience was not so nice, but applauded him immoderately, and encored three of his songs.'

Whatever Walpole may have thought of him, Manzuoli's contribution, along with that of Tenducci and others, was invaluable to Wolferl's development as one of opera's greatest contributors.

SCENE FIVE

On the Nannerl Trail

Leopold's view of the English was inconsistent, but nevertheless he found London a fascinating place, and he took his family on a number of sightseeing tours.

Nannerl, whose daily diary is even more inconsistent than her father's opinion of the English, actually wrote more about London than about any other place on the Grand Tour.

NANNERL MOZART'S LONDON DIARY

Transcript of the original:

In London habe ich gesehn den park und ein jungen elephanten, einen esel der hat weiss und cafe-braune striche und so gleich, das man es nicht beser mahlen konnte. Chelsa, das infalitinhaus, westminster bridge, westminsterkirch, fauxhall, ranelagh, Tower, Richmond, in welchen eine sehr schone Ansicht ist und den koniglichen garden, kiw and Fulham bridge; das wasser werk und ein kamel; westminster hall, lord perong Trial, marlebon; Kensington, in welchen ich den koniglichen garden gesehen habe, british mauseum, in welchen ich gesehen habe bipliatek, antiquadik von allen sorten vogel, fisch, ungeziefer und fruchten ein besonderer Vogel gennant basson, eine Klapperschlang, ein schleyer von baumrinde und harr von den gefrantz von baumrinde; kinesische schuh, ein modell von den grab Jerusalem; alerhand sachen, die in meer wachst, steiner, indischen balsam, die weltkugel und himmelskugel, ond alerhand sachen; greenwich habe ich gesehen, das infalitenhaus, der Konigin ihr schiff, den Park, in welchen ich eine sehr schone aussicht gesehen habe, London bridge, Paulkirch, Soudwark, Monument, foundling hospital, Exchange, Lincolnsin fielsgarten, Temple Bar, Soumerset hauss.

English translation:

In London I have seen the park and a young elephant, a donkey which has white and coffee-brown stripes and so regular that they could not have been painted better; Chelsea the hospital, westminster bridge, westminster church, fauxhall, ranelagh, Tower, Richmond, where there is a very beautiful view and the royal garden, kiw and Fulham bridge, the water works and a camel; westminster hall, lord perong Trial, marlebon, Kensington, where I have seen the royal garden; british mauseum in which I have seen the library, the antiquities, all kinds of birds, fishes, insects and fruits a particular bird called a basson, a Rattlesnake, a cloak made of treebark and hair fringed with treebark; chinese shoe, a model of a tomb in Jerusalem; all kinds of things that grow in the sea, stones, indian balsam, globes of the world and of the stars, and all sorts of things, greenwich I have seen the hospital, the Queen her ship, the Park, in which I have seen a very nice view, London bridge, St. Paul's church, Soudwark, foundling hospital, Exchange and Lincolnsin fielsgarten, Temple Bar, Soumerset hauss.

Her travel notes, written in a very childish style – possibly unwillingly! – are sketchy, uninspired and full of spelling mistakes – both in English and German! However, in spite of – or because of – this very sketchiness they constitute a delightful and concise gem of a London itinerary for any Mozart questor. Whoever undertakes to follow the 'Nannerl Trail' will do so in the sure knowledge that where Nannerl went, Wolferl was sure to follow.

She records that: 'in London I have seen the park . . .'

Nannerl was probably referring to either St James' Park, Green Park or Hyde Park. It was not uncommon to see tame animals kept in London parks in the eighteenth century.

'. . . Chelsea, the hospital . . .'

The Chelsea Royal Hospital, a home for invalid war veterans, is still situated on the Chelsea Embankment to the west of Chelsea Bridge. It was originally founded by Charles II (Nell Gwyn had a hand in it as well), and built by Sir Christopher Wren. It was completed in 1692.

'. . . westminster bridge . . .'

This was one of only two bridges over the Thames in London itself. It was completed in 1750 but had to be rebuilt in 1854 after having been deemed unsafe.

'. . . westminster church . . .'

This would have been Westminster Abbey, where Handel and Purcell, among others, are buried.

The final journey of Dr Charles Burney, a constant travelling companion in this Chronicle, was also to Westminster Abbey.

'. . . fauxhall . . .'

Nannerl's father describes Vauxhall as being:

> 'situated in a very large garden full of avenues which are all lit up as if it were bright day, with many thousands of lamps which are all enclosed in beautiful glass. In the middle is a kind of open summer house where there is an organ; and music with trumpets, kettle drums and all sorts of instruments is played. On all sides there are covered tables. The lighting at the end of the avenue is like a pyramid, and quite enchanting, so I do not know which way to look.'

Entry to this leisure complex was only one shilling, and Leopold was shocked by the drunkenness of many of its visitors. Handel had been a regular visitor to Vauxhall. Vauxhall is now the area of the south bank of the Thames, at Vauxhall Bridge.

The Italian Walk, Vauxhall Gardens.
Source: from an old print.

'. . . ranelagh . . .'

The Ranelagh Gardens were similar to those at Vauxhall. Leopold describes them as:

> 'not large but pleasing and lit up on Mondays and Wednesdays. In it there is a remarkably large round pavilion with many great chandeliers and wall lights. On one side there are steps leading up to an organ on a platform. In the middle there is a great stove where a fire is made when it is cold. Around the stove there are many tables, and in the wall of all the rooms there are alcoves or little chapels, in each of them a table. There are also stairs up to boxes as in a playhouse, and they also have tables. On each table stand all the necessities for coffee and tea drinking. The entrance fee is two and a half shillings per person, and for this

> one has coffee, tea, and bread and butter, and he can eat as much as he wants. It holds up to four and a half thousand people walking about and meeting each other. The ground is covered with a straw platted mat or carpet. Here everyone is equal and no one gives way to a Lord, for his money every man is treated the same.'

Leopold also mentions that at various times music is played.

The Gardens are still situated on the Chelsea Embankment, next to the Royal Chelsea Hospital, although the central pavilion, which was known as the Rotunda, no longer exists.

'. . . Tower . . .'

The Tower of London is one of London's most important historic buildings. In the seventeenth and eighteenth centuries, caged lions and tigers were kept in the grounds, 'At the Tower,' added Leopold, 'the roaring of the lions frightened our Wolfgang.'

'. . . Richmond, where there is a very beautiful view . . .'

Richmond was a town overlooking a bend in the River Thames, a few miles upstream from London. Today, Richmond is a London borough, and still commands a spectacular view of the River, and herds of deer can be seen roaming freely in the enormous Park.

'. . . and the royal garden, kiw . . .'

The Royal Botanic Gardens, known as Kew Gardens, is one of the finest establishments of its kind in the world. They were inaugurated in 1757 by William Aiton, at the instigation of Princess Augusta of Saxe-Gotha, the Queen Mother. Kew Gardens lie beside the River Thames, on the way to Richmond.

'. . . and Fulham bridge . . .'

This is today's Putney Bridge. In 1765 it was a wooden toll bridge, just outside London.

'. . . the water works . . .'

Leopold mentions seeing a machine that draws water from the River Thames to distribute throughout the city during a trip to Westminster.

'. . . and a camel (?); westminster hall . . .'

The manuscript of the Chorus "God is our refuge" by Mozart, in the British Museum.

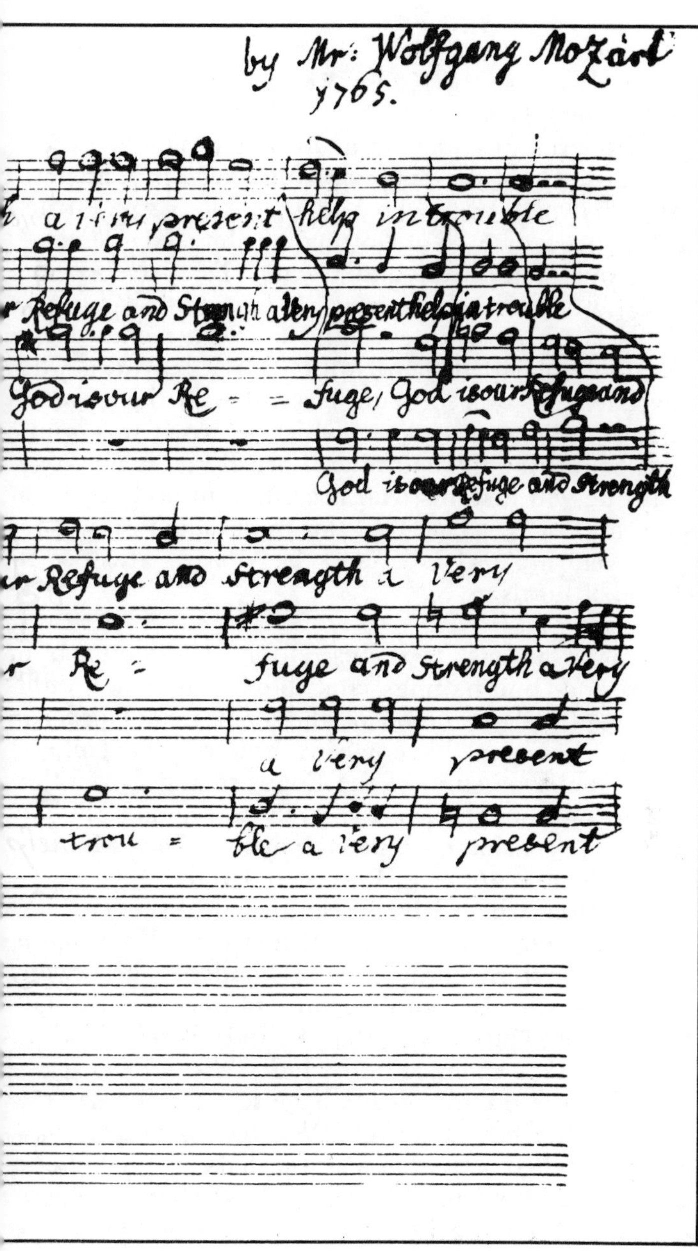

By courtesy of the Trustees of The British Museum, London.

Westminster Hall, the seat of the chief law-court of England, stands beside the Houses of Parliament.

'... lord perong Trial ...'

This is Nannerl's mis-spelling at its worst. The 5th Lord Byron – great-uncle of the poet – was involved in a dispute with a Mr Chaworth over who had the more game on his land during the course of a Nottinghamshire Gentlemens' club's night out at the Star and Garter. Tempers became frayed, and Lord Byron challenged Mr Chaworth to a duel, in which the latter received a wound fourteen inches deep. Horace Walpole recorded the details: ' Mr. Chaworth, who was an excellent fencer ... made his will with the greatest composure, and dictated a paper, which allows it was a fair duel, and died at nine this morning. Lord Byron is not gone off, but says he will take his trial according to precedent, in the House of Lords.' The trial for manslaughter was a sensational event in April 1765, and the Mozarts attended it at the House of Lords.

'... marlebon ...'

Marylebone Gardens were used for dog-fights, bull fights, bear and bull-baitings and boxing matches, and today is Regent's Park, home of the Zoological Gardens. Nannerl may, however, have meant Tyburn, the gallows which stood at the junction of the Edgware and Bayswater Roads, roughly where the Marble Arch now stands. Public hangings were considered entertainment. The Mozarts witnessed public executions in France and Italy.

'... Kensington, where I have seen the royal garden ...'

Nannerl was referring to the gardens of Kensington Palace, on the western peripheries of London. These were laid out in 1725, with beautiful avenues of trees and a small ornamental lake known as the Round Pond. Today, Kensington Gardens is joined onto Hyde Park.

'... british mauseum in which I have seen the library, the antiquities, of all kinds of birds, fishes, insects and fruits a particular bird called a basson, a Rattlesnake, a cloak made of treebark and hair and fringed with treebark; chinese shoe, a model of a tomb in Jerusalem; all kinds of things that grow in the sea, stones, indian balsam, globes of the world and of the stars, and all sorts of things ...'

The British Museum is a significant repository of

antiquities from all over the world. At the time of the Mozarts' visit, it had only been established for twelve years, and was in a state of disorganization. Today's building stands on the same site as the original Montagu House, in Great Russell Street. Although it was open to the public, entry was restricted, and children were not admitted. The Mozarts, however, viewed it as privileged visitors. A number of Mozart's original publications are to be found in the British Museum, including copies of the *four Sonatas, K6–9*, that Wolfgang had written for Mme Victoire and the Comtesse de Tessé in Paris, as well as a first edition of a set of *six Sonatas for clavier, violin or flute, and violincello, K10–15*, which he had written for – and dedicated to – Queen Charlotte. Most significant, however, is the original manuscript of a *Chorus by Mr. Wolfgang Mozart 1765* for four voices. There is also a copy of a J B Delafosse engraving of the Carmontelle water colour of the Mozart family; Leopold had a number of these made in Paris for distribution as publicity material.

'. . . greenwich I have seen the hospital, the Queen her ship, the Park, in which I have seen a very nice view . . .'

Nannerl refers to the Greenwich Naval Hospital on the river, built by Sir Christopher Wren in 1694 on the site of the Tudor palace. The hospital was converted into the present Royal Naval College in 1873. The Mozarts would also have seen the Observatory in Greenwich Park; and the many vessels that would have been moored in the Thames at Greenwich included the royal ship.

'. . . London bridge . . .'

This was the other bridge in London. In 1765 London Bridge was an enormous, sturdy stone structure. 'If you stand on London Bridge and look at the ships,' wrote Leopold, 'you think you are looking at a forest because of all the masts.'

'. . . St Paul's church . . .'

This is St Paul's Cathedral, built by Sir Christopher Wren between 1675 and 1711, with its distinctive dome, modelled on designs by Bramante and Michelangelo.

'. . . Soudwark . . .'

This is the Borough of Southwark, which lies at the southern end of London Bridge.

'. . . Monument. . .'

The Monument to the Fire of London of 1666 stands at the north end of London Bridge.

'. . . foundling hospital . . .'

In 1739, Captain Thomas Coram established the Foundling hospital in Bloomsbury, for mothers and their illegitimate children. The site is roughly where Corams Fields Playground is now situated, between Russell Square and Gray's Inn Road.

'. . . Exchange . . .'

The Royal Exchange, situated next to the Bank of England, was London's international money market. 'Here each nation had its own place,' wrote Leopold. 'Here are the merchants of France, Holland and Spain, and there the German, Italian or Portuguese.'

'. . . Lincolnsin fielsgarten . . .'

Lincoln's Inn Fields is a park situated between Holborn Viaduct and Kingsway. Today, Lincoln's Inn is associated with the legal profession.

'. . . Temple Bar . . .'

The Temple Bar and the Royal Courts of Justice are situated in the Strand, just to the south of Lincoln's Inn.

'. . . Soumerset hauss . . .'

Somerset House, on the south side of the Strand was later rebuilt as a repository for archive material, including births, marriages and deaths.

Somerset House in 1755.

Source: from an old print.

SCENE SIX

There's No Business Like Showbusiness

Thomas Arne, the composer of *Rule Britannia*, was born in London in 1710, and was educated at Eton and Oxford, where he gained a Doctorate in Music, having mastered the flute and the harpsicord. His first opera, *Rosamund*, which he put on at the Lincoln's Inn Fields Theatre in 1733 – was a great success and assured him a safe and secure career in the field of opera and oratorio, albeit in the shadow of his more illustrious contemporary, Handel. He also taught Dr Charles Burney, musician, traveller and writer. From 1742 he was the resident composer at Drury Lane, and, during the 1760's, mounted concerts at various venues, especially at the Little Theatre, Haymarket.

The Little Theatre ran regular seasons of theatrical productions; in the gaps between seasons it was hired out to various fringe groups, novelty acts, as well as Dr Arne's concerts. Dr Arne may well have had a hand in arranging the concert that was given there by the Mozart children on February 21st, 1765.

Some of the programmes mounted at the Little Theatre were more sophisticated than others. Likewise, some audiences were more sophisticated than others, since they were made up of a mixture of upper and middle classes – unlike the French audiences, who were almost exclusively nobles. The emergent British Empire saw a much faster rise in England of the middle classes than in France, or indeed in the rest of Europe, with many fortunes bound up in India and the West Indies. This newly-enriched segment of society understood the meaning of money much more than their titled counterparts, and London saw a new breed of theatre-goer, one which demanded value, often in the most strident tones. It was, therefore, not uncommon for minor riots to take place, leaving the theatre in a shambles.

The incident is recorded of a 'singular entertainment' that took place in the Little Theatre fifteen years before the Mozarts' concert. The advertisements stated that:

> 'at the conclusion of the evening, Monday, January 26th, 1749, the exhibitor, after many unprecedented feats of leger-de-main, would, in sight of the audience, compress himself within a Quart Bottle on the stage, and sing in it! The house overflowed and waited till 8 o'clock, but no bottle conjurer made his appearance, for having secured the money received at the door, he availed himself of his necromantic skill to decamp undetected, leaving the deluded and enraged audience to vent their displeasure on the building, the interior of which they nearly demolished. The hoax was said to have been contrived by the Duke of Montague and other wits of his acquaintance in order to ascertain how far the credulity of the public might be imposed on.'

It appears from this incident, and others like it, that it was possible to impose considerably on public credulity, and Leopold certainly made use of all current advertising techniques for his childrens' concerts. The wording unashamedly owes more to the circus than to culture, with phrases like: 'it is hard to say whether his Execution upon the Harpsicord, and his playing and singing at Sight, or his own Caprice, Fancy, and Compositions for all Instruments, are most astonishing.' Audiences were wooed by invitations to 'try his surprising capacity by giving him . . . any music without Bass, which he will write upon the spot without recurring to his Harpsicord.'

Fortunately for the Mozarts, Wolfgang certainly fulfilled all promise, the concert was a success and the building remained intact, even though Leopold complained that: 'on account of the number of entertainments, it was not so well attended as I had hoped.'

Perhaps he was being optimistic, since the season was in

full swing at the time, with many entertainments to choose from. Nevertheless, he took 130 guineas, with expenses of 27 guineas.

In 1767, the Little Theatre was extended and renamed the Theatre Royal Haymarket. It is still there today.

London was in the lead in Europe as far as public concerts were concerned. These were pioneered by one John Banister in the 1670s, and now, a century later, they were actively promoted by J C Bach, Abel and Dr Arne, among others. Concert Rooms, like those in the Spring Gardens and Hickford's in Brewer Street were mushrooming everywhere, and it was in this fine hall, fifty feet by thirty, with its convex, patterned ceiling, panelled walls, arched windows and a gallery, that the 'Prodigies of Nature' gave their final formal London concert on May 13th.

On June 5th Wolferl was visited by the Hon Daines Barrington, F.R.S. (1727–1800), an eccentric lawyer and man of many disciplines. He had written a number of papers for the Royal Society, and had elicited an interest in Wolfgang during the course of his researches into child prodigies. The interview resulted in a paper, and his observations were published in the *Philosophical Transactions of the Royal Society* in 1769.

After this Leopold was caught up in the more commercialized aspects of the London scene, lowered his sights disgracefully, and pandered to some of the baser instincts of showbusiness. He hit upon the idea of opening his lodgings in Frith Street between twelve and three every day, where for a 'reduced' fee of five shillings, the public could enjoy a private recital by the children. Furthermore, they were encouraged to test Wolferl's ability to perform his usual tricks of improvising on any tune, or playing with his hands covered with a cloth.

They could even come away with copies of Wolferl's sonatas and other compositions – of which there were many by now, as well as engravings of the Carmontelle-Mechel print, all of which were sold at the door.

Throughout June and July, the children performed, 'every Day of the Week, from Twelve to Three o'clock in the Great Room, at the Swan and Hoop, Cornhill. Admittance 2s.6d. each person.'

How long this engagement went on for is not known, but the first advertisement for this venue appeared in the *Public Advertiser* in June, and the last one was dated July 11th, all of which suggest that it was an ongoing occurence of up to six or seven weeks.

The Swan and Hoop no longer exists, but its site is in Change Alley, a winding, twisting alleyway off Cornhill opposite the Royal Exchange. Exchange Alley, as it was then called, was a bustling street of inns, bookshops, insurance offices and the famous coffee houses, where so many international deals were struck over steaming cups of cinnamon-flavoured coffee. The alley still exists, but the layout is changed and the Swan and Hoop is long gone. It stood adjacent to the east edge of Jonathan's Coffee House, the site of which today bears a commemorative plaque.

By July, Leopold had squeezed every last ounce of capital out of London, and he deemed the time ripe to move from a city where drunkenness, prostitution and violence were rampant, recording with disgust the high incidence of riots and street fighting.

'I saw in the street where I live 4,000 men marching past my dwelling . . . in a most disorderly way,' he wrote about the silk riots. He witnessed and described how: 'two blacksmiths fought each other with red hot irons. A large crowd watched as they burned each other on the body. It was horrible.'

Wolfgang, on the other hand, had loved London, and in later years made plans to return. But his plans never came to fruition.

Also the novelty had worn off, the aristocracy had turned to other frivolities, while the middle classes had 'already seen the Mozarts'. There had been further political unrest connected with the American colonies, and there was talk of the King's strange behaviour – the first signs of the porphyria, that creeping genetic disorder that was to progressively destroy King George III.

It had been suggested to Leopold that he should emulate his fellow Germans Handel, J C Bach and Abel, and remain in London. The pickings were rich, and opportunities were there for the right people; but Leopold, on 'mature consideration', decided against it. London had wearied of his family, and he, in turn, had grown to hate London.

'I will not raise my children in this dangerous place, where most of the people have no religion and where one sees nothing but bad examples,' he wrote, perhaps a little too sanctimoniously. 'You would not believe how children are brought up here.'

At the end of July the Mozarts packed fifteen months' worth of luggage.

'It makes me sweat when I look at the amount of luggage we have to pack,' wrote Leopold ruefully. 'We have been in this place for more than a year, it is almost like a home, and going from here needs more preparation than when we left Salzburg.'

On July 24th, the Mozarts left London, arrived in Canterbury that same evening, and spent the night in lodgings. It was here that they were overtaken by the Dutch Envoy, who had heard that they would be stopping off at Canterbury. He had subsequently driven hard to catch Leopold before the family reached Dover. Leopold wrote:

> 'The Dutch Envoy . . begged me to go to The Hague because the Princess von Weilburg, sister of the Prince of Orange (William V) had an inordinate desire to see this child, about whom she had heard and read. Briefly both he and everyone else talked about it so much, and the proposition was so good that I had to come. As you know,' he added wrily, 'one should not refuse a pregnant woman anything.'

Whether or not this last observation was an euphemism by which he meant that it would do the family no harm to aspire to higher social spheres again was immaterial. It sounded, to put it bluntly, like a good deal.

The following day, the Mozarts stopped at Bourne Place, at Bishopsbourne, a village about four miles from Canterbury. They spent the rest of the month there as guests of Mr Horace Mann, whom Leopold had met in London. His uncle – of the same name – was the British ambassador to Tuscany, whom the Mozarts were to meet six years

Bourne Park, Kent.

Source: from owner's postcard.

afterwards in Florence, during their first Italian journey. Horace Mann had rented Bourne Place from a Mr Stephen Beckington. Nannerl loved the place and she wrote that: 'this was a very beautiful estate.'

Bourne Place, now called Bourne Park, is still there in Bishopsbourne.

On July 30th, the Mozarts thanked Thomas Mann for his hospitality, and went back to Canterbury staying there overnight, before attending the horse races at Barham Down Racecourse the following day – Barham Down Racecourse no longer exists.

It was with a light heart that the following day, August 1st, the Mozarts arrived at Dover, and noted with a collective sigh of satisfaction – and relief! – that it was a beautiful day for a perfect crossing.

DAINES BARRINGTON'S REPORT ON MOZART

Account of a very remarkable young musician

Joannes Chrysostomus Wolfgang Theophilus Mozart, was born at Salzburg in Bavaria on the (sic) 17th January 1756.

I have been informed by a most able musician and composer, that he frequently saw him in Vienna, when he was little more than four years old.

By this time he was not only capable of executing lessons on his favourite instrument the harpsicord, but composed some in an easy stile and taste, which were much approved of.

His extraordinary musical talents soon reached the ears of the present empress dowager, who used to place him upon her knees whilst he played the harpsicord.

This notice taken of him by so great a personage, together with a certain consciousness of his most singular abilities, had much emboldened the little musician. Being therefore the next year at one of the German courts, where the elector encouraged him, by saying, that he had nothing to fear from his august presence; little Mozart immediately sat down with great confidence to the harpsicord, informing his highness, that he had played before the empress. . . .

Upon leaving Paris, he came over to England, where he continued more than a year. As during this time I was witness to his most extraordinary abilities as a musician, both at some public concerts, and likewise by having been alone with him at his father's house; I send you the following account, amazing and incredible almost as it may appear.

I carried to him a manuscript duet, which was composed by an English gentleman to some favourite words in Metastasio's opera of Demofoonte.

The whole score was in five parts, viz. accompaniments for a first and second violin, the two vocal parts and a base. I shall here likewise mention, that the parts for the first and second voice were written in what the Italians stile the Contralto clef.

My intention of carrying with me this manuscript composition, was to have an irrefragable proof of his abilities, as a player at sight, it being absolutely impossible that he could have ever seen the music before.

The score was no sooner put upon his desk, than he began to play the symphony in a most masterly manner, as well as in the time and stile which corresponded with the intention of the composer. . .

The symphony ended, he took the upper part, leaving the under one to his father.

His voice in the tone of it was thin and infantine, but nothing could exceed the masterly manner in which he sung.

His father, who took the under part in this duet, was once or twice out, though the passages were not more difficult than those in the upper one; on which occasions the son looked back in some anger pointing out to him his mistakes, and setting him right.

He not only however did complete justice to the duet, by singing his own part in the truest taste, and with the greatest precision: he also threw in the accompaniments of the two violins, wherever they were the most necessary, and produced the best effects. . . .

When he had finished the duet, he expressed himself highly in its approbation, asking with some eagerness whether I had brought any more such music.

Having been informed, however, that he was often visited with musical ideas, to which, even in the midst of the night, he would give utterance on his harpsicord; I told his father that I should be glad to hear some of his extemporary compositions.

His father shook his head at this, saying, that it depended entirely upon his being as it were musically inspired, but that I might ask him whether he was in humour for such a composition.

Happening to know that little Mozart was much

taken notice of by Manzoli, the famous singer, who came over to England in 1764, I said to the boy, that I should be glad to hear an extemporary Love Song, such as his friend Manzoli might choose in an opera.

The boy on this (who continued to sit at his harpsicord) looked back with much archness, and immediately began five or six lines of a jargon recitative proper to introduce a love song.

He then played a symphony which might correspond with an air composed to the single word 'Affetto'.

It had a first and a second part, which, together with the symphonies, was of the length that opera songs generally last: if this extemporary composition was not amazingly capital, yet it was really above mediocrity, and shewed most extraordinary readiness of invention.

Finding that he was in humour, and as it were inspired, I then desired him to compose a Song of Rage, such as might be proper for the opera stage.

The boy again looked back with much archness, and began five or six lines of a jargon recitative proper to precede a Song of Anger.

This lasted also about the same time with the Song of Love; and in the middle of it he had worked himself up to such a pitch, that he beat his harpsicord like a person possessed, rising sometimes in his chair.

After this he played a very difficult lesson, which he had finished a day or two before: his execution was amazing, considering that his little fingers could scarcely reach a fifth on the harpsicord.

His astonishing readiness, however, did not arise merely from great practice; he had a thorough knowledge of the fundamental principles of composition, as, upon producing a treble, he immediately wrote a base under it, which, when tried, had a very good effect.

He was also a great master of modulation, and his transitions from one key to another were excessively natural and judicious; he practised in this manner for a considerable time with an handkerchief over the keys of the harpsicord.

The facts which I have been mentioning I was myself an eye witness of; to which I must add, that I have been informed by two or three able musicians, when Bach the celebrated composer had begun a fugue and left off abruptly, that little Mozart hath immediately taken it up, and worked it after a most masterly manner.

Witness as I was myself of these extraordinary facts, I must own that I could not help suspecting his father imposed with regard to the real age of the boy, though he had not only a most childish appearance, but likewise had all the actions of that stage of life.

For example, whilst he was playing to me, a favourite cat came in, upon which he immediately left his harpsicord, nor could we bring him back for some considerable time.

He would also sometimes run about the room with a stick between his legs by way of a horse. . . .

Mozart's father did not impose with regard to his age when he was in England, for it was in June 1765, that I was witness to what I have above related, when the boy was only eight years and five months old.

I have made frequent enquiries with regard to this very extraordinary genius since he left England, and was told last summer, that he was then at Salzbourg, where he had composed several oratorios, which were much admired.

I am also informed that the prince of Salzbourg, not crediting that such masterly compositions were really those of a child, shut him up for a week, during which he was not permitted to see any one, and was left only with music paper, and the words of an oratorio.

During this time he composed a very capital oratorio, which was most highly approved of upon being performed. . . .

The Rev. Mr. Mainwaring (in his 'Memoirs of

Handel') hath given us a still more apposite instance, and in the same science.

This great musician began to play on the clavicord when he was but seven years of age, and is said to have composed some church services when he was only nine years old, as also the opera of Almeria, when he did not exceed fourteen.

Mr. Mainwaring likewise mentions that Handel, when very young, was struck sometimes whilst in bed with musical ideas, and that, like Mozart, he used to try their effect immediately on a spinnet, which was in his bedchamber.

I am the more glad to state this short comparison between these two early prodigies in music, as it may be hoped that little Mozart may possibly attain to the same advanced years as Handel, contrary to the common observations that such 'ingenia praecocia' are generally short lived.

I think I may say without prejudice to the memory of this great composer, that the scale most clearly preponderates on the side of Mozart in this comparison, as I have already stated that he was a composer when he did not much exceed the age of four.

His extemporary compositions also, of which I was a witness, prove his genius and invention to have been most astonishing; least however, I should insensibly become too strongly his panegyrist, permit me to subscribe myself, Sir,

Your most faithful
humble servant,
Daines Barrington.

ACT

4

MER D'ALLEMAG,
MER DU NORD
Bree Veerthien
Embouchure de la Thamise
Norwich
Yermouth
Oldton
Orfort
Douvre
Pas de Calais
la Haye
Meuse R
Goeree
Brouwershaven
MIDDELBOURG
Vlessingue
Ostende
Dunkerque
Graveline
Calais
Zuyder Zee ou Mer de Sud
Utrecht
Nimmegue
Breda
Lillo
ANVERS
GAND
Bruges
Loevain
BRUXELLES
Maestricht
Deventer
Lochem
Cleves

PRELUDE

Travellers in Flanders have often noted a certain light that lies over the flat countryside that is quite unique, especially during the colder months of the year. There is, under certain conditions, a certain brownness of the soil and a tinted luminosity in the air that bears witness to so much of the work of the old Dutch masters, especially with respect to their use of light in many of their masterpieces.

It was nearly two years since Leopold Mozart had stood transfixed before a triptych of *The Last Supper*, by Dierick Bouts, in St Peter's Church in Louvain on the way to Paris; and now, as he retrieved his coach from the King's Procurator in Calais, in whose care he had left it, he was hardly to know what visual treats were in store for him in the months ahead.

Once more, the Mozarts lodged with M. Dessin at the Hotel d'Angleterre. This time Leopold booked in for two nights, since there was much to be done at Calais before heading north towards the Low Countries and a new court to conquer. He arranged for a large trunk full of furs and winter clothes to be sent on to Grimm's in Paris, since his luggage had grown very considerably during the family's stay in London.

Leopold had raised his social sights once more, and had resumed patronizing the nobility after his fruitful albeit dubious spell of commercialism during the family's last weeks in London. Consequently, the Mozarts met the Duchesse de Montmorency and the Prince de Croy, an important official, dignitary and socialite. He had achieved much to improve the fortunes of Calais after the Peace of 1763. With an eye on English visitors, he was largely responsible for developing the town as a major port, draining the surrounding marshlands, building canals and improving facilities. He was also a genial host who enjoyed mixing the business of arranging travel permits with the pleasure of social intercourse by inviting distinguished visitors to his residence.

Among his guests on August 2nd, were the Mozarts, who enchanted the Prince with their playing on the clavier, especially when Wolfgang and Nannerl played a duet together. After their performance the Prince insisted on summoning violinists to play dance music, and the evening finished with 'un beau bal'.

The Mozarts also called on M. Collet, the organist at the church of Notre Dame, which they had visited on their previous visit to Calais. The church is still there.

On August 3rd, the Mozarts, once more in their own coach, continued their journey along the Flemish coast, past Gravelines to Dunkerque, in the Austrian Netherlands, where they put up at St Catherine's Inn. Dunkerque was a large and populous town with spacious streets, neat and tidy houses and a Bourse. Under the Peace of 1763, the superb fortifications had to be demolished. 'It pains me,' wrote Leopold, 'to see such fine works that cost so much money totally demolished.'

But there were compensations. Thomas Pennant was also there, four weeks after the Mozarts. 'I saw there several smuggling vessels loaded with tea or coffee, brandy, etc, ready to sail for England,' he noted.

The following day, the Mozarts continued to Bergue, where they called in at the church of St Martin and met the organist, M. Blackre. It is not clear where they spent the night of the 4th, but by the 5th they had reached Lille, which an unidentified contemporary travel writer described as the Paris of the North. They booked in at the Hotel Bourbon, in the Grande Place, which was run by M. Cousin.

The post road from Dunkerque is the D916 to Bergues, Cassel and l'Hazewinde, at which point it becomes the D933 to Bailleul, Armentières and Lille.

The Mozarts were held up in Lille for a whole month, because first Wolfgang, then Leopold became ill. Wolfgang had contracted a heavy catarrh, and may well have been admitted to hospital, although Leopold seems loath to admit this possibility in his letters.

'In Lille Wolfgang was filled with a very heavy cararrh and when after a fortnight he was better then my turn came. This took four weeks, and I was not very well when I left Lille.'

The symptoms, in both cases, were a high fever, catarrh, and a very sore throat. Leopold also writes that he suffered from dizziness and, 'had to lie outstretched on the bed, and when I tried to sit up, so everything went round and round, and I vomited.'

Both father and son were attended by a Dr Merlin, and mention is made of an apothecary in La Petite Place.

On August 26th the family were told of the death of the Emperor, Francis I. He was succeeded by the Archduke Joseph, who now became the Emperor Joseph II, and reigned jointly with his mother the Empress Maria Theresia. The family not only recalled their first heady visit to the Austrian court at Schönbrunn three years previously but also, the sad death of the Infanta Isabella, the young heir's wife, when the Mozarts were in Paris.

Nannerl, no doubt very bored with little to do except help her mother look after the two sick males of the family, or have a look round Lille, waxed comparatively eloquent about the town. She recorded visits to a monastery and the Great Hall.

Dr Burney, in his account of his 1772 European tour, writes that in Lille:

> 'the military affords considerable amusement; there are not at present above four batallions, or two thousand men, quartered in the city; though it is usual for the garrison to consist of ten thousand. The mounting guard upon the Grande Place . . . is, in itself, a gay and entertaining sight . . . it is but just to observe likewise, that the French military music is now not only much better in itself, but better performed than it was a few years ago.'

Considering that all this took place right in front of the

Hotel Bourbon, one can imagine how the sick Leopold must have reacted to the sound of marching feet and the strident tones of the bands; he had seen fit to comment on the endless parades that took place right in front of the Goldenen Waldhorn in Ludwigsburg; and when he was ill the previous year in Chelsea, he had even silenced his own son's clavier playing.

Nannerl saw fit to give the parade a passing mention in her diary; being in good health, and of an age to begin appreciating manly qualities, she probably agreed with:

> 'a very intelligent English officer, who was with me [Burney] on the parade, who remarked the same improvement in the discipline, dress, and appearance of the French troops in the same space of time. The men are now select, the manoeuvres shortened, and there is some appearance both of the gentleman and the soldier, even in the common men.'

Finally, Nannerl went on to note a visit to the romantically named Place de la Nouvelle Aventure.

Perhaps the name was portentous, for this was certainly a new adventure, and on September 4th, the family continued their journey to the Hague. Leopold, though still not fully recovered, deemed himself fit enough to travel – if only to get away from the parades and the bands, and the Mozarts left Lille and France behind, and crossed the frontier back into the Austrian Netherlands.

SCENE ONE

Carillons

The family reached Ghent, the capital of East Flanders, on the night of September 4th, and stayed at Saint Sebastian's hotel in the Parade Plaats.

The hotel had been the guildhouse of the Brotherhood of St Sebastian, and originated in the fourteenth century. This Brotherhood of archers was named after St Sebastian, who himself had died, martyred by being tied to a tree and shot with arrows. In 1737 the house eventually became a post hotel and retained the name of the archers' patron saint. The building was demolished at the beginning of the twentieth century, but the site is in the corner of the square which today is known as the Kouter, specifically where the public library stands, adjacent to the Opera House.

In Aachen, nearly two years previously, Wolferl had his first taste of the Flemish predilection for mechanical, jangling sounds, when he found the streets festooned with windchimes made of bits of glass. In Ghent, he was shown this device in its most sophisticated form – the carillon in the tower of St Bavo's Cathedral.

A carillon is an instrument made up of tuned, cup-shaped bells, which are struck by hammers. It is operated from a keyboard, and is often touch sensitive. The earliest examples of carillons date back to the sixteenth century, in Amsterdam; although the practice of making music from the sound of bells goes back even further, when one person merely hit a row of bells with a hammer – somewhat like one would play the tubular bells.

Eventually, mechanical devices were invented, barrels studded with specially placed pegs, which activate certain bells at certain times as the barrel goes round – a principle used in musical boxes. It is also used in that other famous feature of Dutch ingenuity, the barrel-organ, still a very popular feature frequently found in the streets of Holland and Belgium. Some are automatic, while others are operated by turning a crank handle.

The seventeenth and eighteenth centuries saw the apex of carillon building in the Netherlands, with such names as Joris Dumery, Pieter Hemony and Andreas van den Gheyns in the forefront of their casting and manufacture. Most Flemish cities boasted fine carillons, which were housed in the bell towers of churches and cathedrals. The best instruments were those in Bruges, Antwerp, Louvain, Mechelen and, of course, Ghent itself.

Not everyone likes carillons. Dr Burney's introduction to the carillon was in St Bavo's. He climbed the steps of the tower to inspect the machine, and called it:

> 'a Gothic invention, and perhaps a barbarous taste, which neither the French, the English, nor the Italians have imitated or encouraged . . . for by the notes of one passage running into another, everything is rendered so inarticulate and confused as to occasion a very disagreeable jargon.'

This early technology enabled carillons to be used as bellchimes that tolled the hour – and some chimes were far more complex and convoluted than others. Dr Burney continues that in his opinion, – 'to hear the same tune played every hour, in such a stiff and unalterable manner, requires that kind of patience, which nothing but a total absence of taste can produce.'

Operating a carillon, with its combination of playing a keyboard and manipulating machinery, was no mean feat and required a certain amount of physical strength. Dr Burney, despite his opinion of the noise produced by the carillon, was nevertheless suitably impressed by the technology as well as by the skill of the carilloneur 'in his shirt with the collar unbuttoned, and in a violent sweat.'

It is said that Wolferl played the carillon in St Bavo's Cathedral, but whether he was strong enough to actually play a machine that makes a grown man in shirt sleeves sweat violently is doubtful. We can perhaps assume that he had a go.

Although the carillon in St Bavo's in Ghent has been dismantled, the bells are still there in the belfry.

Whether or not Wolferl liked the sounds of the carillon is not known. It is a fact that his ear was very sensitive, and that he hated harsh and distorted sounds as well as instruments that were out of tune. He had a particular loathing for the mechanical organ, a curious little device that had been gaining popularity in some spheres.

'I have made up my mind to compose the Adagio for the clockmaker,' wrote Mozart in 1790, referring to a commission that he had received for the *Adagio and Allegro in F minor K594*, the *Fantasy in F minor K608* and the *Andante in F K616*, all for mechanical organ, 'but as it is very hateful work for me, I have unfortunately not been able to finish it. I compose a bit every day, and I have to stop because it bores me. But I still hope that I shall be able to force myself to finish it little by little. If it were for a larger instrument and the work would sound like an organ piece, then I might enjoy it. However the works are only little pipes which sound too high-pitched and too childish for my taste.'

He also wrote some works for the ethereal sound of a glass harmonica, notably an *Adagio in C* for harmonica, flute, oboe, viola and cello, as well as an *Adagio and Rondo in C minor and major* for the same line up. He shared an interest in this device with Prince Charles of Lorraine.

The whole family climbed up into the bell tower of St Bavo's, and Leopold commented on the spectacular view of the whole of the city from its heady heights. Nannerl commented that it was 326 steps high. From this vantage point, the Mozarts saw the Town Hall opposite, and perhaps even caught a glimpse of Ghent Castle, a foreboding and grim edifice surrounded by a moat, the ancient seat of the Counts of Flanders. The Castle was originally built in 1180 by Philip of Alsace, and from its thick ramparts he was able to keep his restless population subdued. Today it is one of the city's main attractions. It is open to the public and contains, among other curiosities, a somewhat gruesome museum of torture.

The cathedral itself is an imposing example of Flemish

Gothic architecture. It contains a number of examples of Flemish art, including Rubens's *The Miracle of St. Bavo.* The magnificent 1432 altarpiece – of which the lower left panel is missing, having been stolen in 1934 – is attributed to Jan and Hubert van Eyck. It also contains examples of the ubiquitous black and white marble, which Leopold commented upon as a fine feature of Flemish and Dutch churches throughout the Netherlands.

It is possible that Wolferl played the organ in the cathedral, though this is by no means certain. An organ that he did play was in the monastery of the Bernadines at the Baudelo.

The Baudelo is no longer there, but the site is a block adjacent to St Jakob's Square. Opposite St Jakob's Church is the old city library in the Ottogracht, and next to it the Athenaeum gymnasium, which is on the corner of Baudelostraat. At the other end of this road there is a little park on the right, with some basic sports facilities in it. Overlooking this little park is a school – which is the actual site of the old monastery.

The Baudelo organ had been salvaged. It was dismantled and installed in the Grote Kerk, in the Markt, Vlaardingen, a suburb of Rotterdam. It is still there to this day.

On September 6th the Mozarts set off for Antwerp, the City of Rubens.

The organ of the Baudelo in Ghent, now at the Grote Kerk in Vlaardingen, Netherlands.

Photo by courtesy of Bram van den Berg.

SCENE TWO

The City of Rubens

'The whole of Antwerp,' wrote Edward Holmes, 'may be considered as one vast monument of the genius of Rubens, whose name is almost as much identified with architecture and sculpture, as is his hand acknowledged by the judge of painting.'

The Mozarts travelled on to Antwerp along what is now the N70, passing through St Niklaas. They arrived in the evening of September 6th, booked in at the Post Hotel, probably the Ville de Brussels, in the Meirstraat, and stayed for two nights.

The city had a very deep effect on Leopold, in more ways than one. 'It would be impossible to describe the present depressed condition of the former great merchant city of Antwerp and the reasons thereof,' he wrote.

He had a good point, since enumerating the reasons for Antwerp's decline in depth would mean lengthy accounts of contemporary European power struggles.

Briefly, Antwerp is situated well inland on the River Schelde, whose long and wide estuary is combined with what is in effect the Rhine delta complex to the north; all of which makes the coastline in that region resemble a broken biscuit. The city had been one of the most important seaports in the Netherlands since mediaeval times, and had grown rich on the wool trade as well as on the fruits of European Empire building from the sixteenth century onwards. During the course of a long and turbulent series of wars, the southern Netherlands – what is now virtually Belgium, were kicked about like a political football by the Spanish, the French and the Dutch, with only brief periods of stability between.

The Treaty of Westphalia, which brought an end to the Thirty Years' War in 1648, and, specifically, the Peace of Munster, stipulated that the estuary of the Schelde remain closed. It had been closed since 1585 and controlled by the United Provinces – what is Holland today. The frontier established at that time is to all intents and purposes the frontier between Belgium and Holland as it is today, with access from Antwerp to the sea passing through Dutch jurisdiction. The southern Netherlands had been an Austrian province since 1713.

Deprived of access to the sea, Antwerp was ruined, and went into decline. Rubens himself, who was a diplomat as well as an artist, commented that Antwerp was: 'languishing like a consumptive body, declining little by little,' while over a hundred years later, Leopold noted sadly that 'the extraordinarily fine Bourse, or money market, was dead, and the offices of the East and West Indian Trading Companies were empty.'

Burney describes Antwerp as:

> 'a city that fills the mind with more melancholy reflections concerning the vicissitudes of human affairs, and the transient state of worldly glory, than any other in modern times: the exchange, which served as a model for Sir Th. Gresham, when he built that of London, and which, though still entire, is as useless to the inhabitants as the Coloseo at Rome: The Town House (i.e. Hotel de Ville), constructed as a tribunal, for the magistrates, at the head of two hundred thousand inhabitants, which are now reduced to less than twenty thousand: the churches, the palaces, the squares, and whole streets, which, not two hundred years ago, were scarce sufficient to contain the people for whom they were designed, and which are now almost abandoned: the spacious and commodious quays, the numerous canals, cut with such labours and expense, the noble river Scheldt, wider than the Thames at Chelsea-reach, which used to be covered with ships from all three quarters of the world, and on which now, scarce a

> fishing boat can be discovered: all contribute to point out the instability of fortune, and to remind us that, what Babylon, Carthage, Athens, and Palmyra now are, the most flourishing cities of the present period, must in the course of time, inevitably become!'

Antwerp's recovery was slow in coming.

On the Sunday Leopold took his family to Mass at the Cathedral.

'We stayed two days in Antwerp because of Sunday,' wrote Leopold. 'Wolfgang played on the great organ in the cathedral.'

The gothic Cathedral of Our Lady is the biggest church in all the Netherlands, and was built between 1352 and 1535. It is instantly recognizable on the skyline of the city by the fact that out of its two towers, one is unfinished, its building aborted. This was due to the rise of Protestantism in the sixteenth century, and the subsequent religious struggles precluded any further work on it.

The cathedral has been renovated a number of times, but the organ, built in 1891 by P Schyven is not the same instrument that Wolferl played, although the case, created by Erasmus Quellin and P Verbrugghen in 1657, is the original. The organ nowadays rates as one of Europe's premier instruments, and is regularly used in recitals and recordings.

However, Dr Burney saw fit to comment that every organ in Antwerp was out of tune, and his opinion of the local musicians was colourfully put: he describes the violinists augmenting the sound of the organ in the churches as: 'mere scrapers', the bassoon players as: 'worse than those nocturnal performers, who, in London, walk the streets during the winter, under the denomination of 'waits', while the serpent was: 'not only overblown, and detestably out of tune, but exactly resembling the tone, that of a great hungry, or rather angry, Essex calf.'

Edward Holmes, who shared with Dr Burney a hearty dislike for carillons, is very scathing about the carillon in Antwerp's cathedral. He writes that:

> 'without entering the churches, the critical musical faculty is provoked every quarter of an hour by a profane march, which the carillons in the tower of the Cathedral never fail to perform, I suppose for the amusement of the numerous jackdaws who have there found 'their coign of 'vantage', and who, though out of the pale of the church, and without benefit of clergy, might be treated with something better in tune. The hideously inharmonious jangling of these bells, the lamentable attempt at harmonizing a melody, infuses a spirit into the heels somewhat at variance with the tranquility with which one would otherwise loiter round this old and honorable city.'

Nevertheless, today carillon recitals on the cathedral's famous instrument are given regularly.

Leopold's opinion of carillons is not recorded, although he approved of Flemish organs. 'One finds good organs in Flanders and Brabant,' he wrote, 'but above all one would talk about the remarkable paintings. Antwerp in particular is the place for these. We have visited all the churches and I have never seen more black and white marble and such a superabundance of excellent paintings, particularly by Rubens, as I have seen here and in Brussels. His *Descent from the Cross* in the great church in Antwerp surpasses all the rest.'

This Rubens tryptich is arguably the most significant painting to be seen in the city today, along with its counterpart, the *Elevation of the Cross* as well as the *Assumption*, behind the high altar.

The Mozarts could only see these masterpieces on the Sunday; which was the one day on which they were unveiled and put on display.

A statue of Rubens stands in the Groen Plaats, adjacent to the Cathedral, and his tomb in the church of St Jakob, is dominated by his altarpiece, *Virgin and Child with Saints*.

There are a number of churches in Antwerp which are a regular treasure trove of Flemish art, as well as the numerous examples of the black and white marble so beloved by Leopold, especially the churches of St Carolus,

St Paulus and St Andrew.

Nannerl, no doubt influenced by her father's eulogies, waxed exceptionally eloquent about Antwerp, and wrote in her diary of 'the church of Our Lady [cathedral], the Bourse, St Jacob's Church, a monastery, the ramparts, the Carmelite church where the silver Our Lady is, and the chapel of white and black marble . . . the battlements and the Rathaus with bas-relief, the Jesuit church [St. Carolus], the Dominican church [St. Paulus].'

SCENE THREE

At the Court of William of Orange

In 1751, William IV of the House of Orange, the Stadtholder of Holland, as the Netherlands was then officially known, died. He was succeeded by his infant son – who was to become William V on coming of age. In the meantime, his mother, Anne of Hanover, daughter of King George II of England, acted as regent until her own death in 1759. The office of regency was assumed by the dashing and distinguished soldier, the Duke of Brunswick. It was he who effectively ruled the Netherlands from behind the scenes, in the knowledge that the teenaged heir to the title of Stadtholder was in fact a weak and ineffectual character.

It has been said that God created the World in six days, but the Dutch are still creating Holland. It is true that the topography of the coastal regions of the northern Netherlands is constantly changing as a result of the numerous estuaries silting up – with more than a little help from the Dutch. Because of the prevalence of estuaries in the region, which had to be crossed by ferry, Leopold was advised to leave his own carriage in Antwerp and continue the journey by scheduled post coaches – and barges.

It is very difficult to reconstruct with any real degree of accuracy the routes and exact crossing points along this part of the Mozart trail, which must now become ambiguous due to this ever changing topography.

Soon after leaving Antwerp, the coach headed north and crossed into Holland.

The Maas Estuary is in fact the final, convoluted stretch of the Rhine before it empties into the North Sea; there were two crossing points, one at the Willemstadt and one at Moerdijk. The Mozarts took the latter one, leading through

Stadtholder William V of Orange.

By courtesy of Gemientearchief, the Hague.

Princess Caroline of Nassau.

By courtesy of Gemientearchief, the Hague.

Breda, Dordrecht and into Rotterdam, crossing by ferry from Moerdijk to Strijen. Here, Leopold wrote that: 'on the other side are coaches ready to drive one to Rotterdam, where one takes a seat in a small boat and is taken almost to the inn. It was a full day's journey from Antwerp to Rotterdam, that is from half-past six in the morning until eight o'clock in the evening.'

The closest route to the original post road is the E22 motorway all the way from Antwerp to Rotterdam. Just before the bridge over the Maas Estuary there is an exit to Moerdijk, two kilometres from the motorway.

Moerdijk today is a small commercial harbour town. It commands a full-bodied panoramic view of the wide river mouth from a small headland, with the province of South Holland on the other side.

Most of Rotterdam – the section that is relevant – lies on the north side of the river. The whole city was virtually razed to the ground in the Second World War, and there is nothing Mozart-oriented left standing, with the possible exception of the Schielandhuis, in the Korte Hoogstraat, with the tenuous connection of being the only seventeenth century building to have survived the Second World War. It is now the City Museum, and contains some interesting information about dykes and land reclamation.

'In Rotterdam we only stayed half a day,' wrote Leopold, 'because in the afternoon we took a trekschuit (open barge) to the Hague and were already there at 7 o'clock . . . and I will only observe that I had the pleasure of seeing the statue of the famous Erasmus of Rotterdam in the square of that city.'

Erasmus still stands in front of the completely rebuilt Church of St Lawrence, surveying the Grote Kerkplein.

'The usual way of travelling in most parts of the United Provinces,' wrote Thomas Nugent in 1778, 'is in trekschuits, which are large, covered boats, not unlike the barges of the livery companies of London, drawn by a horse at the rate of three miles per hour.'

Leopold who liked to travel 'noblement', probably rented the 'roef' for the family's comfort. This was the covered deck-house of the barge, containing 'a table in the middle with a long drawer, filled with pipes. There is also a spitting box and a little iron pot containing burning turf, for accommodating smokers with a light. The seats are covered with handsome cushions. The roef is generally occupied by the genteeler passengers.'

There is to this day a canal linking Rotterdam with the Hague, although the A13 autobahn runs parallel to it.

Vlaardingen is a small town to the west of Rotterdam, situated just off the A20 motorway. It is virtually a suburb. The Mozarts did not visit Vlaardingen, but it contains an important item of Mozartiana: the organ from the Baudelo monastery in Ghent, on which Wolfgang played. It is now housed in the Grote Kerk, in the Markt.

The organ was built by Pieter van Peteghem (1708–87) and installed in the Baudelo on March 3rd 1764 – hence Leopold referring to it as the 'new church organ in the Bernardines,' since at the time Wolferl played it, it had only been there for a matter of six months. When the Baudelo was demolished, the organ was bought in 1822 by the Grote Kerk in Vlaardingen, where it was installed and restored by Abraham Meere (1761–1841), since it had suffered at the hands of the French when they overran Ghent after the Revolution of 1789.

In The Hague, the barge docked very close to the inn, La Ville de Paris, with which Leopold was not very impressed – possibly due to its proximity to the canal, with its attendant odours. He referred to it as 'une très mauvaise auberge'.

The hotel no longer exists, but the site is at the corner of Korte Houtstraat and Kalvermarkt. The section of canal has also now been filled in, although evidence of a waterway can still be made out opposite.

The Koninklijke Schouwburg, or Royal Theatre, situated in the Korte Voorhout, used to be the residence of Princess Caroline of Nassau-Weilburg, Stadtholder William V's elder sister, at whose urgent invitation the Mozarts had come to the Dutch capital.

The Princess, who was eight and a half months' pregnant at the time, was herself an ardent music lover who spent part of her time at her husband's residence in Kirchheim-bolanden, in the Rhineland, where she maintained an orchestra that performed nightly. When Wolfgang spent an idyllic fortnight there with Aloysia Weber in the winter of

The "Ville de Paris" in the Hague.

Source: from an old print.

1778, Maria Anna Mozart, in a letter to her husband, wrote that Princess Caroline was a: 'passionate lover of music and plays the clavier and sings.'

From the Ville de Paris it was not far to walk to Princess Caroline's residence, so on September 12th Wolfgang and his father walked to perform for Princess Caroline. Nannerl did not go with them on this occasion, since she had been feeling under the weather ever since the family's arrival in The Hague. 'But my daughter,' wrote Leopold. 'was not with us. For now came her turn and she had a very heavy cold in her chest.'

The programme is not known, but the Princess thoroughly enjoyed Wolferl's performance, and found him a delightful little boy. She made a great fuss of him, and gained his loyalty and affection that was to last into the years to come. She not only requested another performance for September 18th, but also recommended him to her brother. The seventeen year old Stadtholder, who was to come of age the following year, took his sister's advice, and requested a performance, even going so far as to send a carriage to fetch Wolferl and his father.

The exact date of the recital for Prince William V of Orange is not known, although Leopold wrote to Hagenauer on September 19th that they, 'were twice with the Princess and once with the Prince of Orange, who had us collected and sent home in his carriage.' It could have been any time from September 13th to 17th.

The palace at which Wolferl played is the Royal Palace in the Lange Voorhout, not far from Princess Caroline's residence.

Within the space of just over one week, the Mozarts' Netherlands mission was accomplished. Princess Caroline of Nassau-Weilburg had seen Wolfgang, had heard Wolfgang, and had been duly conquered by Wolfgang. And Leopold was pleased to report that 'the journey here has been paid for.'

Then, Nannerl's 'cold' took a turn for the worse.

SCENE FOUR

Disaster!

Leopold wrote that the cold in Nannerl's chest was only now beginning to loosen, which was ominous – since it was symptomatic of the beginnings of typhoid. Nannerl's condition did not improve, and by September 26th she was very ill; by the evening she was shivering and feverish, and was suffering from a sore throat. Leopold was by now extremely worried, and had realized that Nannerl's illness was more than just a cold in her chest.

He also had a second worry: he had arranged for Wolferl to give a concert at the Oude Doelen Hall for the following day, September 27th. The *Leydse Courant* ran an article in which the concert was advertised –

> 'The celebrated musician J.G. Wolfgang Mozart of Salzburg, is here at the moment, who is but eight years of age, and most marvellously performs the most difficult concertos and solos by the most famous masters as well as several of his own. This young musician has exhibited his excellent talents at the court of the Stadtholder and in other places exciting the admiration and the applause of all.'

Leopold's quandary was whether to let the concert go on, or to cancel it in order that the family should be together at this critical time.

In the event, Leopold postponed the concert till the 30th, and sent for Doctor Haymans, who was physician to the Imperial, Portuguese, Spanish, French and Neapolitan Envoys. Doctor Haymans prescribed bleeding, and milk and water, as well as various laxatives.

'To cut a long story short,' wrote Leopold, 'she was bled at four o'clock in the evening of September 28th, and although her pulse improved somewhat, she was still a little feverish.'

Since Nannerl appeared to have rallied somewhat, Leopold decided to let Wolferl's postponed concert go ahead as planned, at the Oude Doelen Hall on September 30th. Needless to say, it was a great success. The programme is not known, except that it consisted entirely of Wolferl's own compositions.

The Oude Doelen Hall, or the Old Archers' Hall, is no longer there, but the site is in the Tournooi Veld, near the corner with the Lange Houtsraat. Today the site is occupied by a bank. The developers, aware of the historic significance of the site, have decided to keep the bas-relief in colour of St George and the Dragon, dated 1625, on the front of the building. Sint Joris – St George – was the patron saint of the Doelens, who were a guild of archers similar to St Sebastian's counterparts in Ghent.

In the meantime, Princess Caroline gave birth to Wilhelmina Louise on 28th September.

Sometime during the autumn the Mozarts moved out of the Ville de Paris, and took lodgings with a M. Eske, a clockmaker, in the Spui. The date is not known. M. Eske's house is no longer there, but the site is a department store on the corner of Kalvermarkt and Spui. A plaque in one of the entrances acknowledges this fact.

The Mozarts had not intended to spend a great deal of time in the Netherlands. They had counted on being back in Paris by the time the weather became colder, which was why Leopold had sent a trunk full of furs and winter clothes on to Paris in the first place. But now, Nannerl's condition began to deteriorate seriously, and it looked as if their stay in The Hague would have to be extended.

By October 21st, Dr Haymans decided that Nannerl was dying. A horrified Leopold sent for a priest, and the little girl was given the Last Rites, while the family gathered round, prayed and spoke to her soothingly about the happiness she would find in the next world. And all the while, Dr Haymans had been attending to Nannerl, dosing

The Palace of Princess Caroline van Nassau in the Hague, in eighteenth century and now.

Sources: 18th c: from an old print. 20th c: Załuski photograph.

her with 'balsaam of Smyrna', as well as various other potions and laxatives, none of which had any curative effect whatsoever. It was now becoming evident that his medical skills were not what they were made out to be – despite his distinguished diplomatic clientele.

Finally Leopold exploded.

'I lost all my patience. I said that my daughter declined daily and that she was now no more than skin and bone and it was not the time to be giving her laxatives.'

In the meantime, Princess Caroline, on learning of Nannerl's predicament, summoned her own physician and sent him along to see if he could do anything. Dr Thomas Zwenke was an old man who no longer practised medicine, but at Princess Caroline's instigation, he gave Nannerl a very thorough examination, before questioning Dr Haymans in detail. The bewildered and inept Dr Haymans tried to bluff his way out of the questioning, and gave a series of wrong symptoms to justify the treatment he had been prescribing, hoping to blind Leopold with strings of Latin words.

This was a mistake on his part, since Jesuit-trained Leopold knew Latin well, and saw through his attempts at self justification. He challenged Dr Haymans' false diagnoses and symptoms, and gave Dr Zwenke the correct ones. It was then that the old man realized that Nannerl was suffering from typhoid.

Consequently, Leopold sent Dr Haymans packing, and Dr Zwenke took over, which was very fortunate. Princess Caroline was delighted to hear that, under the old physician's tender care, Nannerl slowly rallied, and her recovery was assured. Leopold, his mind considerably eased, began thinking about moving on, when, on November 15th, Wolferl himself became seriously ill with typhoid, bringing the situation back to square one.

Once again, Dr Zwenke was sent for, and this time Leopold and Maria Anna spent their time nursing their second child.

'Wolfgangerl was attacked on the 15th November by an illness,' wrote Leopold, 'which in 4 weeks has left him in such a pitiful condition that he is not only unrecognizable but has nothing left but his fragile skin and his little bones.

For the last five days we have carried him daily from his bed to a chair.'

By the end of the month Wolferl was dangerously ill, with a very high temperature. He was delirious, his tongue was as dry as wood, his lips were black and swollen, and he was thin and emaciated.

However, by December 1st the crisis appeared to have passed, and Wolferl spent the following week sleeping practically the whole time. He ate very little, and hardly said a word. At the end of that time, he rallied, feeling much better. He even became restless, and expressed a wish to write music, so Leopold placed a board across his bed, and Wolferl spent the greater part of his recovery composing.

This episode, in which both Wolferl and Nannerl came very close to death, is often seen as a serious indictment on Leopold for putting his children through the trials of a major European tour lasting three and a half years without thinking of the physical harm that might result. It is true that the children, especially Wolferl, did suffer to some extent with their health on a number of occasions. Wolfgang himself was never in excellent health, and his early death has often been indirectly attributed to the trials his body must have gone through during his formative years.

At the same time, eighteenth century Europe was a hard, disease-ridden place, where only the very fittest survived, What was more, The Hague, and indeed most of the maritime regions of the Netherlands, were heavily water-borne lands, criss-crossed by canals and river estuaries that served for anything from transport to sewage and water supplies. It was inevitable that water-borne diseases, such as typhoid, would be permanently rampant.

Be that as it may, Wolferl and Nannerl did receive the best that the Netherlands had to offer, since Dr Zwenke was a competent physician, and Princess Caroline, despite her confinement, had proved to be a good and supportive friend. What the outcome would have been if the children had been ill out on the road, or in a court where conditions were unenlightened and primitive, no one can tell.

On the other hand, Wolferl's total dedication to his craft had grown from strength to strength. Even during his sister's illness, when Leopold and Maria Anna sat constantly beside her bed, watching and praying, he would spend hours in the other room composing, and now, having hauled himself out of a virtual coma, he could hardly wait to return to his manuscript paper.

'As a child and a boy you were more earnest than childish,' wrote Leopold to his twenty-one year old son in 1778, 'and when you sat at the clavier or were otherwise intent on music, no one presumed to make the smallest joke with you. Your face was so grave, that many people of insight, on seeing the early flowering of your talent and your earnest little face, wondered how long your life would be.'

Ominous words indeed.

SCENE FIVE

The Müller Organ, Haarlem

In the October of 1765, Wolferl, in Italian operatic mode, wrote the aria *Conservati fidele, K23* as well as his *Fifth Symphony in B flat, K22*; and in January he wrote a set of Variations in G on *Laat ons Juichen, Batavieren! K24*, by Christian Ernst Graaf, the kappellmeister to the Dutch court.

What Graaf made of the fact that a precocious nine year old had knocked up a set of variations on his theme is open to speculation, since there are two contrasting attitudes to this phenomenon: some composers understand and appreciate the skill that this shows, while others see it as an affront – especially if the original theme is not as good as the variations. This latter attitude tends to be the result of jealousy, although it is perhaps understandable if a composer's prized and worthy work is thus put through the mangle – especially by a child. Wolfgang encountered both attitudes in the course of his life. Improvising on a theme has come a long way since Mozart's day, when it was considered to be a quite exceptional skill. Today improvising is very common, especially among jazz and rock musicians, to whom it is second nature.

In the eighteenth century, many composers were unable to improvise in any way at all, and wrote their music more by laborious working out than by instantaneous flair. The contrast in the music of Mozart and some of his contemporaries is often evident in this very spontaneity: where the second rate composer's melodies and harmonies often plod along in a four-square, academically correct sort of a way, that of Mozart flows naturally and effortlessly, and the listener is transported along a musical path that is original, creative and seemingly improvised.

On January 22nd, both children gave another concert at the Oude Doelen Hall, and on the 28th the Mozarts continued their journey to Amsterdam. Leopold decided to go by coach instead of a barge, since 'by mail coach it takes six or seven hours. By water it takes longer.'

The motorway is as close as any other road to the Mozart trail.

In Amsterdam the Mozarts stayed at De Gouden Leeow in Warmoesstraat. Today this is a slightly sleazy little back street, running parallel with the Damsgracht, behind De Bijenkorf department store. Damsgracht is a wide shopping thoroughfare which leads from the Dam, right in the city centre. The inn used to be the third house along on the left, and is no longer there, but the whole section now constitutes the back of De Bijenkorf.

The day after their arrival the children gave the first of their three concerts in Amsterdam. This took place at the Salle de Manège, which was the hall of the Riding School. The concert was a great success, and made a good profit.

Once more, the Riding School is no longer there, but the site is in the vicinity of the Leidseplein end of the Leidsegracht.

Leopold then arranged a second concert for February 26th, but since this was already in Lent, he had to obtain a special dispensation to mount a concert. This was accorded without too much trouble since, it was decreed by the Calvinistic magistrate, '. . . the publishing abroad of the marvellous gift of this child serves to the glory of God.'

This theocratic magnanimity must have caused Leopold to smile wrily, as his strong prejudice against all things Calvinistic battled with his delight that the concert was given the go-ahead.

Once again, the concert was a great success. As with both concerts, all the music consisted of Wolferl's compositions, and both children played duets on one or two claviers – and at the second concert, Wolferl also played the organ. On both occasions, copies of Wolferl's compositions were sold at the door: Leopold had learned much about business enterprise while in London, and no opportunity to cash in an extra florin or two was to be missed.

The "Gouden Leeow" in Amsterdam, prior to demolition.

By courtesy of Gemientearchief, Amsterdam.

Shortly after this concert, Leopold took the children to Haarlem in order to collect from a publisher there his *Violinschule*, his treatise on violin-playing, which he had had translated into Dutch and printed.

'The publisher came to see me,' he wrote, 'and respectfully handed me the book. With him was the organist who invited our little Wolfgang to play on the famous great Haarlem organ. This happened on the following morning from 10 till 11. It is an excellent instrument with 68 stops. Note, these are entirely of pewter, for wood does not last in this damp country.'

They spent the night at Het Gulden Vlies in the Grote Markt, which is still there; and the following morning Leopold took Wolferl to the vast and imposing Grote Kerk opposite.

The Müller organ in St Bavo's Church, or the Grote Kerk, must have been an awesome sight for a little boy to gaze up at, and any little boy other than Wolfgang would certainly have been intimidated by its vastness and magnificence. It is without doubt one of the world's premier instruments. Originally started in 1735 by Christian Müller, the organ was finally finished in 1738, with the carving done by the sculptor Jan van Logteren, and painting and gilding by Hendrick van Limborch. It was restored first in 1866, and again in 1904, and once more between 1959 and 1961. It is now regarded by organists as arguably the finest organ in the world, and is extensively used for recitals and recording.

'Indeed it is the lion of the place,' wrote Dr Burney of the organ, 'but to hear this lion roar is attended with more expense than to hear all the lions and tigers in the Tower of London.'

Dr Burney had to pay the organist half a guinea, and his bellows-blower half a crown to hear its strident tones. However, by tradition, today the entry to these recitals is free.

After their brief excursion to Haarlem, the Mozarts returned to Amsterdam, and then back once more to The Hague, and resumed their lodgings with Mr Eske the watchmaker, in the Spui. They arrived in time to attend the inauguration of William V as Stadtholder on his eighteenth birthday on March 8th.

The title of Stadtholder was given to Holland's head of state. Like so many titles in Europe in the eighteenth century, it possessed special peculiarities. Holland was not a kingdom, but a semi-autonomous federation, and the Stadtholder was in effect the Mayor and Chief Magistrate that held the seven provinces together. The title was the hereditary right of the House of Orange, which had its origins in the old Roman town of Orange in southern France.

William V was weak willed, and throughout his tenure was dominated by the powerful Duke of Brunswick. The latter arranged for him to marry Princess Wilhelmina of Prussia the following year, thus forging himself a strong ally in the blood line of the Dutch court.

William was more interested in art than in affairs of state, and his marvellous collection of Dutch paintings can be seen at the William V Art Gallery at 35 Buitenhof, which is in effect a continuation of the Spui. The gallery is situated opposite the magnificent Binnenhof complex, which overlooks the Hof Vijver ornamental lake, in the centre of The Hague. It was at the Ridderzaal, in the Binnenhof, that William V's inauguration ceremony took place.

Leopold proudly presented the new Stadtholder with the beautifully engraved translation of his *Violinschule.*

Princess Caroline also commissioned six sonatas from Wolferl to mark the occasion, 'From Amsterdam we went back to The Hague for the festival of the Prince of Orange,' wrote Leopold, 'when our little composer was requested to write six sonatas for clavier with violin accompaniment for the Prince's sister, the Princess von Nassau-Weilburg. They were immediately engraved. Also he had to write something for the Prince's concert and an aria for the Princess.'

The *Sonatas* are the set *K26-31.* Princess Caroline liked them enormously, and fondly recalled them in 1778, when she met Mozart again in Kirchheimbolanden.

The Prince's concert was presumably the one at which Wolfgang played on March 11th, and the 'something' he had to compose was the *Galimathias Musicum, K32,* a suite of eighteen pieces scored for clavier, two violins, viola, bass, two oboes, two horns and a bassoon. The work may well have been performed by the court orchestra. The aria –

there was only one – was a rewrite of *Conservati fedele, K23,* which Wolferl originally wrote during the previous October. While in Amsterdam, he also wrote a set of 7 Variations on *Willem van Nassau K25*, to go with the variations he wrote on Graaf's patriotic song.

At the beginning of April, Leopold insisted on returning to Amsterdam, stopping again at Haarlem en route.

'We met a Salzburger in Amsterdam,' he pointed out, 'who had for certain reasons become a Calvinist. I wanted nothing more than to lead him back to the right path. I took great pains. That brought me back to Amsterdam and kept me longer in Holland.'

Apart from this messianic mission, the success of which is not documented, the children gave one more concert at the Riding School on April 16th, for which the entrance fee, as before, was two florins.

The Mozarts also befriended and dined with a certain Mr Donker, who lived near the Bourse. Mr Donker was a merchant, and the Mozarts met him once again in Naples in 1770.

While visiting Amsterdam, the Mozarts went sightseeing, and saw the Town Hall, the offices of the East and West India Companies, the Dutch and Portuguese Synagogue . . .

'The Synagogue of the Portuguese Jews, a handsome but plain building,' wrote Pennant that same year. 'Three men sang extremely well, but the chorus of the whole congregation was the rudest and most horrid outcry I ever heard.'

. . . and the Arsenal, as well as the tall ships docked in the port of the Zuyder Zee, as the IJsselmeer was then called. . . .

'Saw the port,' wrote Pennant, 'which was of great size and crowded with ships.'

. . . and, of course the canals.

'They have the common fault of all canals in this city,' wrote Pennant; 'the water stagnating and growing very offensive.'

The following morning the Mozarts finally turned south, with their sights set once more on distant Paris.

The Salle de Manège, Amsterdam.

By courtesy of Gemientearchief, Amsterdam.

SCENE SIX

Paris revisited

On the evening of April 17th, the post coach pulled up outside the Plaets Royal Hotel in Utrecht, and the Mozarts were welcomed by the proprietor, Sieur Mos. The following morning, Leopold set off early to obtain permission from the city authorities to mount a concert. This was granted, and Leopold duly placed an advertisement in the local paper.

The concert took place in the Muziekzaal at the Vrieburg in the late afternoon of Monday, April 21st, at which both children performed.

The venue is no longer there, since the topography of the whole city centre has been completely altered and the site is submerged in a complex, Euro-style development. The centre is now dominated by an enormous shopping precinct with multi-storey car parks, and an adjacent arts complex – the Vredenburg, which houses a number of conference rooms, recital rooms, theatre and concert halls. The Vredenburg overlooks a large, concrete square, with a shopping street opposite. That shopping street is broadly the site of the old Vrieburg, at which the Mozarts gave their concert.

The site of the Plaets Royal Hotel is in the Minrebroeder-straat. The hotel was turned into an orphanage which was demolished in 1876 to make way for the small St Willibrod's church.

Nearby stands the Cathedral, with its imposing tower, the highest in the Netherlands. It is separate from the cathedral proper, and has an archway running under it. Being a Calvinist church, it is doubtful whether Wolferl played its organ, given Leopold's strong anti-Calvinist

The "Plaets Royal" building in Minrebroederstraat, Utrecht.

By courtesy of Gemientearchief, Utrecht.

sentiments, even though the Mozarts did stay in Utrecht for several days.

The exact date that the Mozarts left Utrecht is not known, although they travelled back to Rotterdam, and retraced their wake and wheelmarks, returning by way of Moerdijk to Antwerp.

Little is known of the Mozarts' return visit to the crumbling Belgian city-port, except that the children gave a concert on April 30th, of which there are no details.

Presumably they stayed once more at the Post Hotel in the Meir, where Leopold had left his own carriage on the outward trip. What he did with the coach is not clear, since from Brussels onwards the Mozarts were travelling by mail coach once more, which suggests that he most likely sold his coach, probably in Antwerp.

The Mozarts arrived in Mechelen (Malines) during the first week in May. 'We travelled through Malines,' wrote Leopold, 'where we visited our old acquaintance, the Archbishop.'

The Archbishop in question was Count Johann Henryk von Frankenberg, who held the office of Archbishop of Mechelen from 1759 till 1801. This was the only archbishopric in the Austrian Netherlands, a position that still exists; today the Archbishop of Mechelen also holds the title of Primate of Belgium.

The Mozarts first met him at his Brussels residence while on their way to Paris, when the children played for him, and received presents. This time the family called on him at his official residence, which is still there, beside the Cathedral.

Leopold was very happy to be in Catholic country again after his conscientious tribulations in Calvinistic Holland, and doubtless he and the Archbishop had a great deal to talk about, both on a musical, mundane as well as a theological plane.

The Cathedral of St Rombaud is an imposing Gothic edifice, with a monolithic tower seemingly hewn from solid granite by the elements. It dates back to the middle of the sixteenth century, the time of the establishment of the archbishopric.

The Archbishop took the family to see the cathedral, and Wolferl played the organ, for which he received a dagger as a present. The organ is still there, although it has been moved from its original emplacement.

The Cathedral contains a wealth of black and white marble to delight and elevate Leopold, as well as many paintings by such masters as Snellinckx, van Coxie, Jean de Namur, Janssens, Smeyers, Gaeremyn, the older Lessayve and, of course, van Dyck, whose 'Crucifixion' is the altarpiece in the South Transept. There is also a marble statue to Archbishop Frankenberg commemorating his office. The carillon in the tower is reckoned to be the finest in Belgium.

The Cathedral looks over the top of a row of houses, all of them fronted with a motley array of typically Flemish façades, at the delightful Grote Markt, with its extraordinary Town Hall, in which two completely diverse styles (14th and 16th centuries) 'agree to differ', to dramatic architectural effect.

A walk through Mechelen will reveal a tryptich of the Adoration of the Magi by Rubens in St Jan's Church, as

The Residence of the Archbishop of Mechelen.
Source: Załuski photograph.

well as the old, cobbled and now industrialized van Beethovenstraat, named after the composer's grandfather, who was living there at the time of the Mozarts' visit.

The Mozarts only stayed one night in Mechelen, and on May 8th they continued their journey to Brussels, only a matter of 25km away, where they spent one night, presumably at the Hotel d'Angleterre.

From Brussels to Paris, the Mozarts retraced their outward journey exactly, stopping only at Valenciennes, which they reached at half past seven on the evening of May 9th.

They most probably put up at the post hotel, which was the 'Auberge du Pot d'Etain', which is still there at 95 rue de Quesnoy.

However, they met – and may well have stayed with – Mme Geoffrion, who was the wife of the Director of

Farming, at their residence in the rue des Cardinaux, which today houses the Institut St. Jean Baptiste.

The Mozarts also met Emmanuel Graeb, who was maitre de musique at the chapelle St. Pierre, the local judiciary. He was a musician of renown, and composer of masses, motets and occasional music.

When they stopped in Brussels, Nannerl and her mother had bought some of the beautiful lace that was to be found there, and now, in Valenciennes, they also bought 'some fine cambric linen, one piece smooth and one piece with a flower pattern,' while Leopold noted the intricate clockwork at the Town Hall.

One of the features of modern road travel in the Netherlands, and especially in Belgium, is the sight of church steeples in the distance, with the road seemingly making straight for them. Since the countryside is flat, there is no historical reason for twisting and turning roads, and modern roads tend to follow the old, established tracks and post roads, which generally used distant church steeples as beacons. The effect is similar today. In the eighteenth century the road from Brussels to Paris, at least the French section, was not only paved with cobbles, but was also straight, making a beeline between towns. No doubt these factors were the reason why the mail coach was able to make the long Valenciennes to Paris run – no less than 200km – in just one day – including a stop at Cambrai.

'Then,' wrote Leopold, 'without stopping anywhere we travelled on to Paris and went to the lodgings which our friend Grimm had engaged for us. Thank God, we found our luggage in good condition.'

This last sentence would suggest that one of the banes of today's travel, that of luggage going astray or arriving in tattered condition, may well have been one of the fears experienced by the eighteenth century mail coach traveller as well.

It had been a very long day, and not only the children, but also everyone else on the mail coach, were very glad to have reached their destination at long last.

ACT 5

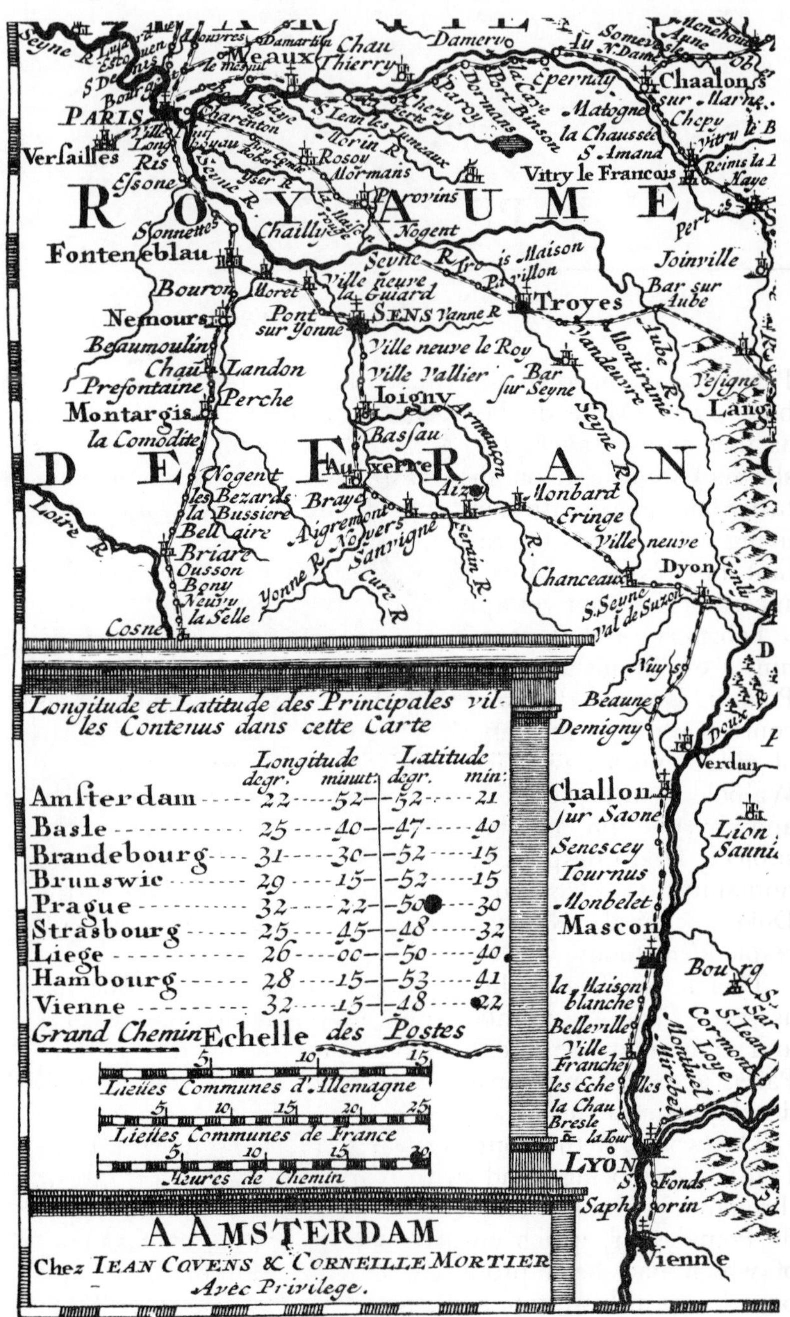
ROYAUME DE FRANCE
PARIS
Versailles
Meaux
Chau Thierry
Chaalons sur Marne
Vitry le Francois
Fontenebleau
Nemours
Montargis
Provins
Nogent
Troyes
SENS
Ioigny
Auxerre
Joinville
Bar sur Aube
Monbard
Dyon
Beaune
Challon sur Saone
Tournus
Mascon
LYON
Vienne
Briare
Cosne
Loire R.
Seyne R.
Yonne R.
Longitude et Latitude des Principales villes Contenus dans cette Carte
Longitude degr. minut. Latitude degr. min.
Amsterdam 22 52 52 21
Basle 25 40 47 40
Brandebourg 31 30 52 15
Brunswic 29 15 52 15
Prague 32 22 50 30
Strasbourg 25 45 48 32
Liege 26 00 50 40
Hambourg 28 15 53 41
Vienne 32 15 48 22
Grand Chemin
Echelle des Postes
Lieües Communes d'Allemagne
Lieües Communes de France
Heures de Chemin
A AMSTERDAM
Chez IEAN COVENS & CORNEILLE MORTIER
Avec Privilege.

PRELUDE

Paris had changed in the two years since the Mozarts had been away. Mme de Pompadour had died the same year as the family travelled to England, and much of the style she had imprinted on the Court with her personality and taste had gone with her. The King, although outwardly living with his wife, ran a series of relatively unimportant mistresses – Mme du Barry, Mme de Pompadour's successor, had not yet appeared on the scene.

February of that year had seen the death, aged eighty-nine, of Stanislas Leszczyński, flamboyant ex-king of Poland, Duke of Lorraine and father of the Queen. 'This court is plunged into another deep mourning for the death of old Stanislas, who fell into the fire', wrote Sir Horace Walpole at the end of February; 'it caught his nightgown and burnt him terribly before he got assistance. His subjects are in despair, for he was a model of goodness and humanity.' In 1778 Wolfgang was to spend ten days in the Duke's capital, Nancy, whose magnificent centre, still resplendent today, was designed and built by him.

The musical and literary scenario was still thriving as ever, and a number of prominent artists, writers and musicians were either living in, or operating from Paris, and exerting considerable influence on the cultural development of Europe.

The works of the controversial François Voltaire (1694–1778) were being read with varying degrees of favour throughout France. He had been a favourite with Mme de Pompadour, which ensured success for his plays, many of which had been produced at court. Although he had been living at his estate at Ferney, near Geneva, since 1758, his spirit, the embodiment of the eighteenth century 'enlightenment' movement was alive and thriving in the capital.

François Gossec (1734–1829) was one of the leading lights in the development of orchestral music, and was later heavily involved with the Concert Spirituel. He was the first Frenchman to write symphonies, and eventually became the Revolution's favoured composer. In common with Stamitz in Mannheim, he propagated the idea of good orchestral technique and tone colour. He founded the Concerts des Amateurs in 1769 in which he achieved a high standard of orchestral performance that was much admired even in Mannheim. It was in Paris that Stamitz himself first heard the clarinet, in a work by Rameau, and introduced it into his own orchestra back in Mannheim – to the admiration of Mozart in later years.

At this time, Gossec was in the employment of the Prince de Condé at Chantilly, outside Paris.

The year that the Mozarts left for England marked the deaths of two prominent French musicians: Jean-Marie Le Clair (1697–1764), one of Paris' foremost virtuoso violinists, was stabbed to death; and Jean Philippe Rameau (1638–1764), France's leading eighteenth century composer, who had originally taken the young Gossec under his wing, died of typhoid. His death left a void in the field of opera, which was filled with the arrival of André Grétry (1741–1813). Grétry was a Belgian by birth, and came to Paris under the exhortation of Voltaire, who rated him highly. His successes were considerable; he had written up to fifty popular operas – lightweight and melodious, if lacking in substance and originality.

The year after the Mozarts finally left Paris, Schobert, Wolferl's early model for violin and clavier sonatas, died as a result of eating poisoned mushrooms.

In the meantime, a group of intellectuals calling themselves the 'Encyclopaedists' had established themselves with a view to editing the Great French Encyclopaedia, which took from 1751 till 1772 to produce. At the centre of this group were Denis Diderot (1713–1784) and Jean d'Alembert (1717-83), with a considerable quantity of musical items written by Jean-Jacques Rousseau (1712–78).

From this vast enterprise had emerged *The Dictionary of Music* in 1767, which went on to become the definitive reference book of eighteenth century music.

And all the while Grimm was editing his *Correspondance Littéraire*, whereby he kept the courts and salons of Europe informed with all the latest literary and intellectual trends.

At the hub of this illustrious circle of French Establishment sat Mme Louise d'Epinay, at her house in the Rue Richelieu. She was a leading literary socialite on the Paris salon circuit, and counted Diderot, Rousseau, d'Alembert and – especially – Voltaire and Grimm, among her closest friends.

Although very much a member of the French Establishment, which Leopold held in some contempt, Mme d'Epinay shared with Grimm the opinion that Wolfgang Mozart was already an important figure in European music, and was instrumental in helping to promote his talents. She was impressed enough to write to her very good friend Voltaire, recommending the young composer for his attention. In later years she was destined to have considerable influence on the life of Mozart.

Mme d'Epinay was not the only influential person that Wolfgang had encountered during his two stays in Paris. Another musician that the Mozarts met was Christian Cannabich (1731–98), on a visit to Paris from Mannheim, where he was the leader of the court orchestra. On this occasion, no significant relationship was struck, although, once again, in years to come, Wolfgang was to forge a strong and lifelong friendship with Cannabich as well as with his wife Lisel, and their daughter Rosa.

The family also met Ignaz von Beecke (1733–1803), a soldier and a fine musician who studied under Jomelli and went on to become kappellmeister – as well as Captain – at the court of Prince Kraft Ernst Oettingen-Wallerstein in Bavaria. He too was to play a part in the Mozart fortunes in the years to come.

The Mozarts' second stay in Paris lacked the glory and adulation of the first; but what Wolfgang lost in fame and personal achievement in 1766 he gained in the seeds that were sown for the future.

SCENE ONE

Pomp and Burgundy Wine

In the rue Traversière, opposite the Clos Georgeot, almost in the shadow of the Palais Royal, there lived a merchant by the name of M. Brie, who purveyed baths. Grimm had arranged for the Mozarts to lodge with M. Brie when they arrived back in Paris on May 10th 1766, after an absence of just over two years.

Nowhere was the length of this absence more evident than when Wolferl and Nannerl once more tried to don their Versailles-style black clothes. They did not fit. Like all children everywhere, they had outgrown their clothes.

'Since here we must again wear black clothes,' wrote Leopold, expressing the perennial problem faced by all parents down the ages, 'one can see how my children have grown.'

The rue Traversière is now largely the rue Molière, but the topography of the area has been considerably altered since 1766. The nearby Avenue de l'Opera had not yet been built, and neither the Clos Georgeot nor M. Brie's house exist any more, although the site is approximately where 12 rue Molière is now.

Grimm was overjoyed to see the Mozarts again, and was delighted with the children's progress. Nannerl had grown from a little girl of twelve to a maturing young lady of nearly fifteen, while Wolferl had changed from little more than a cute infant into a fully fledged boy of ten, even now showing signs of that same sophistication and sense of style that characterized his father.

Three years of constant adulation may well have taken its toll on a young boy's character, and could have turned him into an unlikeable spoilt brat. Among the list of criticisms

Friedrich Melchior Grimm.
Source: from an old print.

endured by Leopold was this very point. To what extent was he entitled to regard Wolferl as a superboy whose place was among the gods? If Wolferl had turned into a spoilt brat it would hardly have been surprising – history is full of wonder children who could not handle their own greatness. Fingers have been pointed at certain aspects of Mozart's behaviour, both as a child and an adult, that have shown him in a bad light. His love of buffoonery can easily be forgiven, as can his intolerance as such of inferior musicians; but many have taken exception to his preoccupation with obscene humour in later years. A number of musicians also objected to his tendency to belittle their work in front of their friends by improvising variations and improvements at the drop of a hat – for that is surely tactless and insensitive.

Grimm's evidence on the Mozarts' return to Paris painted a very different picture of Wolferl: 'he is moreover,' he wrote, 'one of the most loveable of creatures imaginable, who puts wit and spirit into everything he says and does, with all the grace and sweetness of his age.'

Two years is a long time in a child's life.

Two years is also a long time in fashion too, and if Leopold had expected a repeat of the children's runaway successes of the year before yesteryear, he was to be disappointed. Paris had changed considerably since their previous stay. The bourgeoisie and the middle classes were no longer interested in hearing a ten year old and a fifteen year old, no matter how talented they were, while the royal court had stagnated into a style limbo after the death of Mme de Pompadour.

Dr F Gehring writes that '. . . the public appears to have taken a less lively interest in the wonderful children than on the occasion of their first visit to Paris.'

At about this time, Michel-Barthélemy Ollivier (1712–84) painted *Tea at Prince Louis-François de Conti's*, which shows Wolfgang sitting at a harpsichord, with guitarist and singer Pierre Jelyotte behind him, surrounded by the Prince and some guests taking tea. This oil painting now hangs in the Louvre.

'Meanwhile,' wrote Leopold proudly, 'we have had the pleasure of a visit from the Hereditary Prince of Brunswick.

He is a very pleasant, handsome and friendly man, and when he came into the room, he asked me if I was the author of the book on the violin.'

Leopold was singularly flattered by this unsolicited recognition of his *Violinschule* by one of Europe's foremost characters. Prince Karl Wilhelm Ferdinand von Braunschweig (1735-1806) was a soldier who had greatly distinguished himself during the Thirty Years War. He had married Augusta, daughter of the Prince of Wales, and came to Paris that year. He was by all accounts a singularly brave, wise and kindly man, respected by his enemies as well as his allies on the field of battle. He was also a fine violinist.

On hearing Wolferl perform the Prince told Grimm that 'many a finished kappellmeister in the profession might die without having learnt what this boy of 9 knew.'

In 1806 Prince Karl Wilhelm was mortally wounded in battle – aged seventy-one!

The Mozarts went to Versailles twice during their second trip to Paris, first on May 28th when they stayed for four days, and then again in the middle of June. Once more they lodged at Au Cormier in the rue des Bons Enfants.

One of their appearances was for the benefit of the Prince de Condé.

'They played several times at Versailles,' continued Gehring. 'The daughter of the Duke d'Orléans, whom Joseph II wished to marry and who afterwards espoused the Prince de Condé, took the liberty of dedicating a little rondo for harpsicord and violin of her own composition to Wolfgang.'

The Mozarts' meeting with the Prince de Condé turned out to be a fortuitous one. Prince Louis Joseph de Condé (1736–1818) was a distinguished soldier and veteran of the Seven Years' War. He was the Governor of Burgundy, with estates at Chantilly, to the north of Paris. He was very taken with the Mozarts, and invited them to Dijon, the capital of Burgundy.

'The Prince de Condé,' wrote Leopold, 'has engaged us to go there on the occasion of the assembly of the Burgundian states, which only happens every three years.'

The Prince was responsible for improving the industries

and communications of Burgundy, which is an area of France roughly between the Lyons area to the south and Champagne to the north, Alsace-Lorraine and Switzerland to the east and the general area of central France to the west. Today the name is synonymous with the wines of Macon, Beaune and Nuits St Georges.

And so the Mozarts left Paris by post coach on July 12th, the same date as the Prince, to find Dijon sparkling and alive with the excitement of playing host to between 250 and 300 delegates, under the presidency of the Prince himself. The city was in the throes of carnival – with colourful processions and cortèges, everybody in ceremonial dress, as the civil and ecclesiastical authorities gave full vent to all the pomp and circumstance that the city elders could muster. The occasion was, furthermore, a source of considerable income, as large sums of money would be spent in the city – and in the surrounding wine producing regions.

The sessions, or Etats, were officially opened by the Prince on July 14th with the usual display of sumptuous splendour – an auspicious date yet to be for France!

In the meantime, Leopold, at the Prince's instigation, arranged a concert in the Town Hall for July 18th. Posters advertising the event appeared in the city, announcing the concert by the two children, which had been arranged by permission of the Prince de Condé, who would be honouring the event with his presence.

The Mayor and the aldermen arranged for the great reception room to be used as the venue, and spared neither effort nor expense in preparing it for an event worthy of the occasion. The hall was illuminated with chandeliers, lustres and candelabra, and a platform was erected in the middle of the hall, with an armchair covered with crimson velvet placed on it for the Prince himself. All around seating was arranged for his entourage.

At 8 o'clock on July 18th, the Prince arrived at the Town Hall, accompanied by M. de la Tour du Pain, the governor of the province, the Intendant and several other notaries, to be received by the Mayor, the Aldermen, the Commissioner of Police and various civic functionaries and secretaries, all dressed in ceremonial robes and cravats. The Prince was led to his seat on the raised platform, and gave orders for it to be taken down and placed among the ladies!

When everyone was settled, refreshments – no doubt of local produce and good vintage – were brought, and the concert began.

Wolferl and Nannerl were not the only musicians involved in this concert. There were some others, whose merits – or lack of them – were documented by Leopold in his Reiseaufzeichnungen:

Les Musiciens:		
Violini	Sotrau,	très médiocre.
	Fantini,	un miserable italien detestable.
	Paquet	
	Lorenzetti	asini tutti.
	Mauriat.	
alto.	Le brun,	un racleur
Violoncello Baß.	Du Chargé	miserable.
	amidey.	
Fagotto Bassone.	Le Maire	
Hautbois.	deux frères	Rotten.

Despite the orchestra, Wolferl and Nannerl, as well as Leopold and Maria Anna, must all have thoroughly enjoyed the pomp and circumstance of this occasion, even if the Dijon Orchestra lacked the finesse of Mannheim or Württemberg. There was the added knowledge that the Prince had specifically requested the Mozarts' performance simply because he loved their music.

One can take it for granted that the Prince thoroughly enjoyed the occasion too, with some superb music – in the company of the ladies – in the opulent and heady atmosphere of the great reception room of Dijon Town Hall; and where the crimson velvet of the Prince's armchair matched the colour of the Burgundy wine perfectly, as it reflected, in crystal glasses and decanters, the light of a host of twinkling candles.

The old Town Hall is now the Archives Départementales du Côte d'Or, and is at No 8 rue Jeannin, on the corner of rue Lamonnoye. The concert took place in the hall on the first floor, a sumptuously panelled room with an impressively decorated ceiling. A plaque commemorating the concert is built into the floor in front of the great mantelpiece.

Except that the engraver carved the date as July 16th in error.

An extract from minutes taken by a secretary at the Mairie, describing the concert at the Town Hall in Dijon runs as follows:

> The Mayor and the aldermen, having been notified that his Excellency the Prince de Condé wished to attend a clavier concert given by the two young children of the Master of Music to the Archduke of Salzburg, in which the music was to comprise of the compositions of one of these children, aged eight, have prepared for the occasion the great hall, which was bedecked with chandeliers, lustres and candelabra; an armchair of crimson velvet was placed on a platform in the centre of the hall for his Excellency and seating for all the distinguished persons of his entourage was placed all around. His Excellency, having arrived at the Town Hall at eight o'clock in the evening, accompanied by M. de la Tour du Pain, the governor of this province, the Intendant and several other notaries, was received by the Mayor, the Aldermen, the Syndicate, the Secretary and representatives of the Police, all dressed in robes and cravats in the manner of Ponchartin, and was ushered into the hall where, when he arrived, he gave orders for the armchair to be taken off the platform which had been prepared for him, and sat on the benches among the ladies. Then his Excellency was offered refreshments, which he accepted graciously, and likewise refreshments were served to the Ladies and Lords who accompanied him. And after the concert was over, the Prince having risen, was followed by the whole council and accompanied to his carriage, and after he had mounted into it, everyone retired.

SCENE TWO

Homeward Bound

The post road from Paris to Dijon is picturesque, with long stretches off the beaten track, leading through thick forests and hilly wine growing regions, today giving delightful glimpses of the true, provincial and historic France.

The road, initially the N7, leaves Paris through the Porte d'Italie, and continues as far as Fontainebleau, where it picks up the N6 to Sens and Auxerre. This road broadly follows the River Yonne, which it crosses at Pont-sur-Yonne. After Auxerre it follows the N6 for a matter of five kilometres until it reaches the D956 turning to the left. The route continues along the D956 to St Bris-le-Vineux – a village with caves selling wine, St Cyr-les-Colons, Grand Vaucharme, Aigremont and Noyers.

In most cases, the road bypasses the villages, but the original post road naturally went through the centres. Noyers, a superb example of a mediaeval village, largely intact and unchanged, was a local centre in olden days, and an important staging post on the road to Dijon. Entering the town through the mediaeval archway one can easily imagine that little has changed in Noyers for centuries, and that the Mozarts would have seen it much as it is today, with its many old, stone houses with exposed timber frames.

After Noyers, the road leads through Sanvigne and Aisy-sur-Armançon. At Aisy, the road continues all the way to Montbard, crossing the railway and the Canal de Bourgogne. The road then follows the banks of the Canal, which runs parallel to the River Brenne. The route stays with the D905 until it meets the D19 off to the left, which leads through Lucenay-le-Duc, and la Villeneuve-les-

Convers, until it reaches the N71 near Courceau. The N71 leads straight to Dijon, by way of Chanceau, St. Seine-l'Abbaye and Val-Suzon.

Dijon is also the birthplace of Rameau, who would very likely have heard Mozart in Paris. He died in 1764, and his statue stands in the Place de la Sainte Chapelle, which is off the rue Rameau.

During their stay in Dijon, Wolferl and Nannerl may well have given some private recitals, though no specific occasion is recorded. The concert took place at the beginning of their stay, and was well attended by delegates, many of whom would probably have been delighted to invite the children to perform in their homes or lodgings.

Leopold also met Charles de Brosses (1709–77), a music lover and well-known literary figure. He was responsible, among other things, for translating the libretti of Metastasio into French. Mozart used Metastasio's libretti in *Il rè Pastore* and an adaptation of his libretto in *La Clemenza di Tito*. He also used his texts in a number of concert arias, including the two he had written in London and the Hague, *Va dal furor portata*, and *Conservati fedele*.

After a fortnight's stay, the Mozarts set off for Lyon, along what today is the N74, changing after Chagny to the N6.

Thomas Pennant was also on the same road that year, making for Lyon. 'Left Dijon,' he wrote. 'The country on the right hilly, on the left flat and very beautiful and rich. About a mile from the city was a gibbet on which was hung a malefactor, and nearby a wheel with a body on it, broke about 10 months before for sacrilege.'

The road took both Pennant and the Mozarts through some of the most important parts of France's wine growing areas on the banks of the Saône, and the itinerary reads like a veritable vintner's catalogue: Gevrey-Chambertain, Nuits St Georges, Beaune, Macon. 'Passed Baume (Beaune), famous for its wine,' continued Pennant. 'On the right is Volne situated beneath the hills, famed for its wine. The vines in all this country are planted pell mell, and each is supported with a stick. In the middle of the vineyards are planted cherry and walnut trees.'

Leopold, noted for commenting on things oenological,

later wrote to Hagenauer from Lyon, 'You know that I am a fierce drinker of Burgundy wine. Oh how often have I wished to be drinking it in Salzburg with my good friends! It costs so little and one has such a desire for it, that I have often wished to order a vessel holding 240 bottles.'

During this time, the documentation of the dates is somewhat erratic and largely speculative, as are overnight stops, so the exact date of the Mozarts' departure from the Burgundian capital is not known, nor how long it took to reach Lyon, except that on July 26th their coach came down a very steep hill into the city; crossing over the River Saône, they were examined by customs.

'Do not be shocked that I am writing to you from Lyon,' wrote Leopold on August 16th, no doubt assuming that Lorenz Hagenauer would have expected them to make for Salzburg after Dijon.

Leopold was in fact making for Geneva, where he had established contacts, specifically with a letter of recommendation from Mme d'Epinay to visit Voltaire. The route took him well off course, but there was no post road that led directly from Dijon to Geneva; this necessitated a detour through Lyon.

The city was built at the confluence of two of France's major rivers, the Rhône and the Saône. The Mozarts stayed in Lyon for four weeks, largely at the instigation of a merchant and amateur musician whom they met, by the name of Meurikofer. Very little is known about him except that he used to sing a particular Italian song which delighted Wolferl, who liked the way he sang it with his spectacles on the end of his nose – the sort of quirky little detail that so often appeals to children.

'You will no doubt remember him,' Leopold recalled in 1770, when they met again in Naples, writing to his wife, 'a dark young man, who often had to sing that Italian song for Wolfgang with his spectacles on his nose.'

Wolferl requested frequent performances of this *pièce de résistance*!

During their stay in Lyon, Wolferl and Nannerl did perform on at least one occasion. 'On August 13th,' wrote Deutsch, 'they took part in a concert. This concert was one in a series that took place every Wednesday in the hall in the Place des Cordeliers, opposite St Bonaventura's Church.'

The event was a great success, if the takings were anything to go by, since the concert brought in nearly 1,000 livres that day. Tickets cost three livres a head, which suggested an audience of over 300. However, the 1,000 livres would have been shared out among the other musicians who had also taken part.

A notice appeared in the local newspaper that day:

> 'This evening, at a grand Concert, there will be a performance of the ACTE D'HILAS by M. du Bury, sung by Mme Charpentier and M. Lobreau. M.J.G. Wolfgang Mozart, a child aged nine, composer and master of music, will perform several pieces on the clavecin, solo. The concert will conclude with the ACTE DE LA DANSE DES TALENTS LYRIQUES by M. Rameau.'

The Hotel du Concert where the concert took place no longer exists, although the church is still there in the Place des Cordeliers, a matter of a hundred metres from the Pont Lafayette over the River Rhône. The site of the hall is right in the middle of the road, the dual-carriageway Place des Cordeliers, between the church and the river.

Like so many buildings in Lyon at this time, it was Italianate in style, due to the large numbers of Italians living in, and setting the style of, Lyon in the eighteenth century. Most of them were involved in the city's thriving silk industry.

The Hall was originally built by the Italian architect from Milan, Federico Pietra Santa in 1724, and was according to a contemporary account 'a fine edifice of singular taste, whose style recalls that given by the ancient Romans to their temples.'

It consisted of a ground floor and a first floor, which was reserved for the director of music. A vestibule led into the hall and two rooms coming off it, one which served as a library, the other as a dressing room for the artistes. The concert hall itself was shaped like a trapezoid some thirteen by ten metres. There were galleries running along both sides, two metres above ground level. The stage was separated from the auditorium by a ballustrade, and was built up on several levels. It was a small hall, but with a capacity of 250 (it must have been standing room only on August 13th 1766), it was more than adequate to accommodate the patrons from the aristocracy. The hall was destroyed in 1856.

During their stay, the Mozarts made many friends and Maria Anna, Nannerl and Wolfgang had new clothes made; and although Leopold wrote that at present silks were expensive, he added that in Lyon they must appear well dressed.

Lyon saw the most appalling atrocities during the Terror that followed the Revolution, and the Mozarts had a foretaste of times to come, as they witnessed an execution.

On August 18th or thereabouts, the Mozarts left Lyon and made for Geneva.

The post road leaves Lyon by the N84 through Miribel, Montluel and Pérouges until it picks up the N75 near St Denis-en-Bugey, leading north towards Pont d'Ain. However, after about five kilometres it takes the D36 to Abronay. About ten kilometres beyond Abronay it rejoins the N84 – in effect all the same road – and continues towards Nantua. It follows the road through Nantua and St Germain-de-Joux and on to Bellegarde, where it picks up the N206 to Collonges. From here, it becomes the D984 to Farges, St Genis Pouilly, and on to Geneva.

Today this road is built up all the way to Perruges, and even after that, it passes through many villages before reaching the foothills of the mountains after Poncin. Once the gradients begin the road becomes very attractive.

Although the latter part of this road is in the mountains, it is not full of twists, turns and hairpin bends, like most modern mountain roads. After the initial climb, the road follows a broad valley nearly all the way to Geneva, with spectacular views of the mountains to each side. Nearly all post roads in the mountains followed valleys: after all, a team of horses pulling a coach could not cope with anything but the easiest mountain routes with the least steep climbs – and these were few and far between.

To glimpse for the first time the foothills of the Savoy

Alps to the south of Geneva must have brought a lump to the Mozart throats – for this is the beginning of the mighty mountain range that sweeps eastward through the belly of Europe towards the Imperial capital of Vienna – just touching Salzburg with its northern flank.

The Mozarts were homeward bound at last.

SCENE THREE

The Foothills of Elysium

'When you receive this letter,' wrote Leopold from Lyon, 'we shall have had long enough, with God's help, to discover what Geneva and the Genevan pocket watches are like.'

There is virtually no documentation that gives details of the Mozarts' stay in Geneva, only legend and speculation, though most probably based on truth. The only certainties are that they arrived in the city of both Calvin and Rousseau on August 22nd, and stayed for nearly three weeks. It is even likely that they did not actually enter the city, which was in the throes of unrest that had flared up between the liberals and the governing aristocracy. This had come to a head when the latter had burned Jean-Jacques Rousseau's *Emile* – a work critical of dogmatic Christianity and authority. A team of negotiators from France and the Swiss Cantons tried to mediate in the matter, but to no avail, and there was even more trouble in the streets.

Their lodgings, are a matter of speculation, although three possibilities present themselves: firstly, Leopold had a letter of recommendation, most probably from Grimm or Mme d'Epinay, to stay with the painter Jean Huber, who was a close friend of Voltaire. Huber lived in Vernaz, several kilometres south from Geneva on the road to Salève. Secondly, he may have booked in at the Auberge de Secheron, a smart inn at the gates of the city, where all the best people stayed. Thirdly, according to tradition, they put up at the Hotel de la Balance, Geneva's post hotel.

Leopold wrote that 'we found the centre of the city still in flames after the civil war, which did not prevent us from staying three weeks.' In fact, the troubles were not as severe as they were made out, and were probably localised.

'Perhaps you know,' he continued, 'that just outside Geneva the famous M. Voltaire has a castle where he lives, called Ferney.'

Voltaire had bought the estate on the proceeds of some wise speculation and the winnings of a lottery. It was situated in the hills overlooking the Swiss city, only just on French soil. He was officially banned from France – which in effect meant Paris – and chose to live at a convenient point from which he could escape to any one of four independent jurisdictions, should any troublesome situation or censure arise; those of Geneva, Vaud, Sardinia and France. He was now an old man, in feeble health, but kept an open house and an open mind on most things philosophical. His greatest pleasure lay in drama, and he had built a theatre in the grounds of his estate, in which he mounted his own plays for his friends. This was frowned on by the strictly Calvinistic authorities in Geneva, where drama of any kind was banned, and music was severely restricted.

Burney, who travelled to Geneva four years later, commented that: 'there is but little music to be heard in this place as there is no play-house allowed; nor are there organs in the churches, except two, which are used for psalmody only, in the true purity of John Calvin.'

He went on to comment that there was only one composer in Geneva, a certain M. Fritz. All of which placed the Mozarts and their plans to mount concerts at a severe disadvantage.

However, these regulations were frequently flouted, and not only by Voltaire. Even as the Mozarts were staying in Geneva, there was a travelling comic opera troupe in town who seemed to be enjoying some success relatively unmolested. It appeared that the rich, bourgeois inhabitants of Geneva – and the 'enlightened' liberal set who had not taken to the streets – tended to pay lip service to Calvinistic ideals, while continuing, behind closed doors, to lead the middle-class liberal-thinking existences to which they had become accustomed. Consequently they tried to ignore the unrest in the streets, and continued with a pretence that all was well.

Leopold heartily disapproved of Calvinists, and would have eschewed the atheist Voltaire and all his set, had not Mme d'Epinay written to him from Paris, recommending Wolfgang for his attention; so Leopold's conscience was superceded by Voltaire's importance as a literary figure. He took steps to contact the philosopher, offering a concert by his children.

Voltaire, however, was in no mood for listening to children making music, so he declined, giving his poor health as an excuse.

'Your little Mazar,' he wrote to Mme d'Epinay later, 'has chosen, I fear, a bad time to bring harmony into the Temple of Discord. I never go out. I have been very ill when this phenomenon had illuminated the black horizon of Geneva. At last he has departed, to my profound regret, without my having seen him.'

The snub, even if unintentional, had been reinforced by the fact that he was not too ill to place the travelling opera troupe on the stage of his theatre. The troupe had had a modicum of success in the city, so Leopold reckoned that if they were able to make some sort of headway as entertainers, then so should his children.

Having gained while in England considerable experience in promoting his family, he set wheels in motion with his usual enterprising gusto. His gamble paid off, and the Mozarts gave a number of performances in – or in the environs of – Geneva, although no venue is documented. The writer and literary editor Gabriel Cramer, a friend of Voltaire, in a letter, dated September 5th 1766, to Jean-Rodolphe Sinner, a librarian in Berne, wrote: 'We have here a young German who has been strongly recommended to me from Paris; he plays the clavier as no one has played it before; he reads at sight; he extemporizes on all themes instantly, and with that he is gay, childlike, full of spirit. One scarcely dares speak of him for fear of not being believed.'

The 24-year-old Belgian composer André Grétry was in Geneva at the time. Apparently unperturbed by the troubles, he was living near the Town Hall, composing his first opera, *Isabelle et Gertrude.*

'I have recently met in Geneva a child who read

everything in sight,' he wrote; 'his father told me in front of an assembled crowd: so that there will be no doubt of my son's talent, write him, for tomorrow, a very difficult sonata movement. So I wrote him an allegro in E flat, difficult but without affectation. He played it, and everyone, except me, cried at the miracle. The child did not stop, but in following the modulations, he had substituted some of the passages that I'd written.'

Wolferl had tried his trick of instantly improvising, or improving, on other musicians' themes, which in this case was evidently taken in the spirit intended.

André Grétry was duly impressed.

According to legend, the children also performed for Princess Galitzine at her house in Geneva. During their first stay in Paris, the Mozarts had met Prince Galitzine, who so enjoyed the Mozarts' music that he wanted Leopold to bring his talented family to his native Russia.

'Prince Galitzine tried to persuade me to go to Russia,' wrote Leopold, 'but to no avail. Russia is too far off and too cold.'

Having exhausted all possibilities in Geneva, Leopold deemed the time ripe to move on to the Swiss capital, and the family set off along the northern shore of Lake Geneva on September 11th.

'When one wishes to go to Bern one must travel through Lausanne,' he wrote. 'Although we only meant to spend the morning there when we descended from our coach the servants of Prince Louis of Württemberg, of Mme d'Aulbone, of Mme Hermenche, of M. and Mme de Sévery came to us and I had to let these distinguished personages persuade me to spend five days in Lausanne.'

The Prince in question was the younger brother – and heir – of Prince Karl Eugen of Württemberg. He welcomed the Mozarts very warmly to Lausanne, and invited them to stay at le Grand-Montriond, which he was renting from the Crinsoz family. This residence no longer exists. The Prince was also renting the Château de Renens, just outside the town, although he preferred to stay at le Grand-Montriond since it was closer to the centre. The Mozarts may have visited Renens, which still exists, during their stay.

Wolfgang wrote a flute 'traversière' solo piece, *K33a*, for the Prince during his stay in Lausanne, although this piece is now lost.

Lausanne was a complete contrast to the severe and puritanical Geneva. It was a cosmopolitan meeting place of aristocrats and intellectuals, and a melting pot of ideas, fashion, enlightenment and good living. The salon of Mme d'Aulbone was notable for being a centre of conversation and culture, and the meeting place of the Springtime Society, one of several organizations dedicated to free thinking. The following year Mme d'Aulbone became Mme de Corcelles through her second marriage to Jonathan Polier Seigneur de Corcelles-le-Jorat; and it was as Mme de Corcelles that her salon became better known. It was patronized by such local luminaries as M. and Mme de Sévery – who were with the Prince when he welcomed the Mozarts – as well as Dr Tissot, the famous doctor and colleague of Prince Louis who not only wrote a thesis on Mozart, but also took over the tenancy of le Grand-Montriond.

The salon was situated in the Corcelles' apartment in the Place St François. The building, which was an hotel, was demolished in 1896 to make way for the Hôtel de Postes.

Thus, the Lausanneois minds were open not only to new ideas, but also to new people, and strangers of distinction were made welcome. The Mozarts qualified on that score.

During the latter half of the eighteenth century, there was a great deal of building in the beautiful surrounds of Lausanne, and many fine châteaux and rambling estates sprang up, giving the impression that Vaud, with its pleasant climate, was a veritable Eden, both physically and intellectually. Jean-Jacques Rousseau lived in the hills to the north. Prince Louis himself edited a weekly, twelve page newsletter with the bizarre title of *Aristide ou le Citoyen*. It was the organ of the Moral Society, another one of those societies that flourished in Vaud at the time. The society's aims were to edify and enlighten its readers.

The emininent physician, Dr Samuel-Auguste-André Tissot, was a regular contributor with advice on such varied topics as how to preserve good health, or how to be a better, more virtuous person, but for the edition of October 11th of that year, he was asked to write a full dissertation on Wolfgang Mozart.

Fascinated by the boy's amazing talent, Dr Tissot readily accepted the brief, and his ensuing study filled the whole magazine. It is interesting to compare his article with that written in London the previous year by his English counterpart, the Hon Daines Barrington, F.R.S.

On September 15th, the children gave a concert at the Town Hall. The venue was the salle des Deux-Cents, which today houses the seat of the legislative council. An audience of seventy paid the entrance fee of forty sous per head. On September 18th, they gave another performance in the salon of Mon Repos, the residence of the Marquis de Langallerie, a friend of Voltaire.

ARISTIDE OU LE CITOYEN
XVIth Treatise of October 11th 1766

Edera crescentem ornate poetam – VIRGIL
Cast some flowers upon this young artist

I have no doubt, gentlemen, that you have heard the young Mozard (sic) and I am convinced that he will have made the same impression on you as on any one else upon whom Nature has bestowed organs capable of appreciating the creation of fine art. You will have seen with as much surprise as pleasure a nine-year-old child play the clavier like one of the great masters; and it will surprise you even more to learn from reliable sources that he has already been playing in this exceptional fashion for three years; to know that everything he plays is of his own composition; to have found in all his pieces, and likewise in his improvisations, a strength of character which is the mark of genius; that diversity which betrays the fire of imagination, and that charm which confirms a sure sense of judgment; finally to have seen him execute the most difficult pieces with an ease and a fluency that would have been surprising even in a thirty-year-old musician; and you would probably have asked the same question that I have heard asked by many: can you understand it?

It seems to me that there is as much foolishness in being amazed by nothing as in being amazed by everything: to witness phenomena without trying to seek an explanation is a mark of imbecility. I have seen a great deal of our young musician, I have observed him attentively, and I would hazard some thoughts here.

Our little Orpheus was born with a finely tuned ear and a great temperament strongly affected by music; the son of a great musician and younger brother of a sister whose playing has excited your admiration, the first sounds that he heard were those of harmony, whose strings have been resonating within him since his infancy; as soon as they were plucked, he knew that he had to make music. In everyone, that influence which the soul subconsciously exercises through the voice, in a musician it exercises through the fingers, indeed, through the whole body, an instrument so adapted to its needs that he soon becomes familiar with all its usages. At birth, he received an organ so true and delicate that the least discord would be painful. . . . The delicacy and sensitivity of young Mozard's ear are so great that false, harsh or excessively loud sounds make him cry. His imagination is as musical as his ear; it contains multitudes of notes all at the same time; a single note recalls instantly all the other notes which would constitute a whole melodic sequence, or even a complete symphony . . . Sometimes he has been drawn involuntarily, as if by some unknown force, to his clavier, from which he drew sounds that became the living expression of an idea with which he had been preoccupied.

This child is completely natural, he is pleasant, he is knowledgeable on subjects other than music; if he had not been a musician, he would have been a perfectly ordinary boy. If he had not been born the son of a musician, his talent may not have had a chance to develop till later, and all his other gifts would have remained buried.

One may confidently predict that he will one day be one of the very greatest exponents of his art; but there is the fear that, having bloomed so young, might he not mature too quickly? It is true that gifted children have often been spent by the time they are in the prime of life, their overworked muscles having become strained and incapable of further creation; but experience has also shown that sometimes those born with a great aptitude for one of the fine arts have continued creating for a very long time; the disposition that comes with this talent flows with such ease that its expression hardly affects it, and it is obvious that giving vent to his talent does not tire the young Mozard at all.

I have treated long, gentlemen, on the musical child; I would be failing if I were not to touch on the question of the moral child, which it is only right that it should be of interest to you. A well ordered head complements a virtuous soul and gentle manners; the fact of this experience has been verified in many great artists, and young Mozard furnishes us with further proof of this; his heart is as sensitive as his ear; he has a modesty rare for his age, rare for such excellence; one is truly uplifted through listening to him expressing his talents, and concluding with such an amiable candour and a demeanour that suggests it would be unforgivable to take any share of the glory for himself. One cannot see, without emotion, the tenderness that he shows for his father, who remains always dignified, who has taken greater care in the moulding of character than in the cultivation of talent, and who speaks of education with as much conviction as he speaks of music; he is well rewarded by success; it is edifying for him to see his two delightful children more flattered by a look of approbation that they anxiously seek in his eyes than by all the applause of an audience. This single trait seems to me to sum up all three of their characters to their credit, and they offer two reflexions on education which, I admit are not new, except in their application: the one, is that many people who might excel in one genre are only mediocre because that genre is not of their own making; this issue, the first that should be made in deciding on a choice of vocation, is the one that is seldom taken into consideration; instead of trying a child out with different vocations, in the same way as one would touch a metal or a stone to ascertain its nature, the parents would normally suppose that their judgment will suffice to establish this; success would give credence to this principle. The second reflexion would be for fathers of gifted children to imitate the example of M.Mozard who, far from imposing on his son, has always taken care to temper the fires of his own ambitions; the opposite view would always stifle the finest geniuses and even abort the most superior talents.

I have the honour to be, etc . . .

It was Prince Louis himself who described his own, very personal Mozart experience:

> 'When I observe the young Mozart creating his sweet and sublime symphonies, while jesting merrily, they could well be taken for the language of the gods, and all the strings of my very being seem to resound with that very immortality which all the forces of my spirit might desire. Transported by delightful illusions, beyond that narrow sphere which constricts my senses, it would take but little for me to recognize this precious child of heaven for one of those pure geniuses who dwell in that wondrous state which was to become my destiny.'

The style was Elysian, to say the least!

SCENE FOUR

Rhinefall

On September 18th, the Mozarts climbed into the carriage that Leopold had hired to take the family to Berne.

'The Prince was still with us when we took our places in our carriage,' he wrote, 'and, upon shaking hands with him, I had to promise to write to him often and send him news about ourselves.'

That night, the family arrived in Berne, where they spent eight days, during which time, 'we had an opportunity of getting to know men of learning.'

Who these men were, that Leopold referred to, we have no idea since there is no further documentation about the Mozarts' stay in Berne; there is an unconfirmed legend of a concert at L'Hôtel de Musique.

From Berne, the family continued towards Zürich, although Leopold stopped off at Baden, which was the birthplace of his mother, Anna Maria.

Anna Maria Mozart, née Sulzer, was born in the town in Aargau on July 30th 1696, and was at that time still living in Augsburg. Leopold had a low opinion of her, having said, a year before Wolferl's birth, that, 'she is poor and has little sense – it's unfortunately true, even if she were a thousand times my mother.'

Despite this unfortunate opinion of her, he still wanted to show Wolferl and Nannerl the town where their grandmother was born. In the event, the old lady died in Augsburg three months later, on December 11th of that year, aged seventy.

The Mozarts arrived in Zürich on September 28th, and booked in at Zum Schwert or L'Hôtellerie de l'Épée in the Weinplatz, which is still there. Today it is a five star hotel, and a plaque commemorates Mozart's stay.

The children gave two private concerts for members of the Société de Musique de Zürich, a very exclusive organization, whose accounts show a payment of, '28 pounds to the Salzburgeois for symphonies and nocturnes.' The concerts, which were not open to the public, took place in the Music Room of the Worshipful Collegium, on the River Limmat, on October 7th and 9th. For each of the concerts, printed handouts were distributed. After the concerts, Leopold sold copies of Wolferl's compositions.

One of the most important features of the Mozarts' visit to Zürich was their meeting with the Gessner brothers.

Salomon Gessner (1730–88) was a poet, painter and engraver. His work in all three spheres was of the lyrical, pastoral tendency, and his reputation was spread even as far as England, where he was very popular. His pastoral idylls and landscapes – both in words and pictures – were particularly loved by Byron, Wordsworth and Sir Walter Scott.

His brother Johannes, less well-known but nonetheless eminent, was a physicist. Their house was a regular meeting place of poets, writers, painters and musicians as well as men of science and learning. Between them, they made the Mozarts feel very welcome, and their hospitality was much appreciated by Leopold.

'At Zürich,' he wrote, 'the two learned Gessners made our stay very pleasant and our parting very sorrowful. We took away tokens of their friendship.'

The tokens in question consisted of mutual exchanges of works. Salomon presented the Mozarts with a copy of the latest edition of his poetry, with a written dedication, while Leopold presented the brothers with copies of Mechel's engravings of the Carmontelle aquarelle of the Mozarts from Paris; he left quite a number of these in Switzerland. He also left copies of Wolferl's music, with the promise of more to come.

On October 13th the Mozarts set off for Winterthur, where they stayed one night with the town clerk and writer, Wolfgang Dietrich Sulzer, a friend of Salomon Gessner. Sulzer was an excellent flautist and music lover, and welcomed the Mozarts to his house on Salomon Gessner's recommendation. The children played for him as a token of their appreciation for his hospitality.

Although heavily brutalized during the course of the Industrial Revolution, Winterthur had maintained a strong musical tradition dating back to the seventeenth century. In 1629 the Winterthur College of Music was founded, and became one of Europe's premier music academies, which flourishes to this day.

But the Mozarts did not present themselves there, since they moved on the following morning. 'From there we went through Winterthur to Schaffhausen. Here our four days' stay was a very pleasant one.'

It is easy to understand that Leopold enjoyed his stay in Switzerland's most northerly city, for here the family once more met the river that had been their constant companion over a long stretch of their outward journey, such a long time ago. On seeing the Rhine again the Mozarts must have felt the proximity of home territories in the same way as on glimpsing for the first time the western reaches of the familiar Alps on their approach to Geneva. This is a younger, more vigorous Rhine that sallies forth from the nearby Lake Constance; and nowhere is this youthful vigour more spectacularly evident than in the magnificent Rhinefalls on the outskirts of the city – the highest waterfall in Europe. The children must have marvelled at the sight.

Schaffhausen itself is beautifully situated on hills straddling the Rhine, although today much of the city is brutalized by modern industry. Most of it lies on the north bank of the Rhine – an unusual feature, since everywhere else between Lake Constance and the point, just outside Basle, where France, Switzerland and Germany meet, the river forms the boundary between the latter two countries.

It is likely that Leopold visited the Benedictine Abbey, which is now the Church of All Saints, thankful to be among Catholics once more, after an apparently traumatic surfeit of Calvinism and Lutheranism. He always made a point of visiting monasteries whenever he could, either from a spiritual viewpoint, or to see the marvels of that opulent, baroque style so beloved by central European Benedictines; or to show Wolferl the organ. Or merely to secure a night's free lodging!

Once more, lack of evidence causes us to speculate whether or not this was the case in Schaffhausen.

The post road corresponds easily with modern roads in Switzerland. It leaves Geneva by route 1 and follows the north shore of the lake to Lausanne, and continues through Moudon towards Berne. Near Payerne the post road turned to the right, leading into Fribourg, where it picks up route 12 to Berne. In Berne it reverts to route 1 once more, and continues as far as Olten, after which it goes to Aarau and Brugg along route 5. At Brugg it picks up route 3 to Baden and Zürich.

From Zürich to Winterthur it is route 1 again, after which route 15, which merges with the N4 autobahn leads into Schaffhausen. Going north from Schaffhausen, it continues along the N4 to the German border.

On October 19th, as the local grape harvest was in full swing, the Mozarts set off once more for the border with Karl Eugen's – and Prince Louis's – Württemberg, only a few kilometres away.

SCENE FIVE

Birth of a River

It is only a very short distance that separates Europe's two greatest rivers in the eastern reaches of the Black Forest – and at significant points in both their courses as well. At Donaueschingen, some forty kilometres to the north of Europe's premier waterfall on the Rhine, three streams merge to become the official source of the Danube. A typical, golden Autumn adorned the richly forested landscape of Germany's southern reaches when the Mozarts' carriage drew up in front of the Schloss, the seat of the Princes von Fürstenberg.

'We found on our arrival at Donaueschingen Herr Meissner,' wrote Leopold, 'who came to our coach to greet us and helped us with our luggage out of the carriage!'

Joseph Meissner was Leopold's colleague from Salzburg. He was singer, singing teacher and composer at the court of the Archbishop, and like Leopold, he was at that time on leave. In common with Leopold, Meissner was an avid traveller, a pursuit that had frequently landed him in trouble with his employer for overstepping his privileges with extended absences. The Mozarts met up with him on their travels to Italy on a number of occasions.

'He remained in Donaueschingen with us for four days,' continued Leopold.

The Mozarts themselves stayed on at the Schloss as guests of the music loving Prince and his kappellmeister, Franz Anton Martelli. 'The Director of Music, Martelli, came at once with greetings and an invitation to Court.'

The Mozarts had originally met Prince von Fürstenberg in Paris, two years previously, so their reputation was well established.

The official spring of the Danube in the grounds of the Fürstenberg Palace at Donaueschingen.

Source: Załuski photograph.

'His Highness the Prince received us with extraordinary graciousness,' wrote Leopold. 'We did not need to announce ourselves for we were being eagerly awaited, as Herr Meissner can witness.'

They were certainly pleased to see the Prince again, but perhaps the most touching scenario was Wolferl's meeting once again with his former subject of – and emigré from – the Kingdom of Rücken: Sebastian Winter had left Leopold's service to enter the more lucrative employment of the Prince as personal valet while the family were in Paris. Wolferl had been disappointed at the time, having lost a good friend and partner-in-fantasy. Whether or not the two of them now recreated some of their past adventures-in-reverse is not on record, but Sebastian no doubt noticed the considerable changes in his young friend, both as a child and as a musician.

Whatever temporary ill feeling that may have occurred between Leopold and Sebastian Winter in Paris was perhaps justified. After all, Sebastian had found a very attractive post elsewhere, and had left Leopold without a servant; and soon after he had bought him a new livery to boot. But Sebastian had been a good friend and loyal servant to the Mozarts in the past, and any feelings of resentment were soon replaced with understanding; Leopold could hardly begrudge him a better position in a princely house.

What was more, they kept in touch for years afterwards, since Leopold regularly corresponded with Sebastian when forwarding Wolferl's compositions for the Prince, signing his letters, 'I ever remain your honest old friend – Mozart.' Even later, in 1786, Wolgang himself wrote to Sebastian in connection with composing some music for the Prince, opening with, 'Dearest friend! Companion of my youth!'

Sebastian Winter must have been quite an extraordinary character, as a servant, friend and no mean judge of music himself. It is very likely that it was these very qualities that had prompted Prince von Fürstenberg to head-hunt Sebastian as his personal valet – possibly even a 'gentleman's gentleman' or confidant – in the first place.

'Well,' wrote Leopold, 'we were there for twelve days. On nine days there was music in the evening from five to nine, and each time we performed something different.'

The concerts took place in the great hall, and the music hungry Prince worked the Mozarts very hard – there were in fact two concerts each day. However, it is doubtful whether Wolferl or Nannerl minded in the least. Wolferl would have enjoyed the endless music making in the princely Schloss.

It can be assumed that the Mozarts would have attended mass at the Church of St Johann, which is only thirty metres from the Schloss, and it is also very likely that Wolferl may even have played the organ – although there is no hard evidence of this.

All in all, the Mozarts' stay in Donaueschingen had been very pleasant and stimulating, and when it was time to move on, the parting was warm and friendly. 'The Prince gave me 24 louis d'or,' wrote Leopold, 'and to each of my children a diamond ring. Tears flowed from his eyes when we took leave of him, and in short we all cried at the parting. He begged me to write to him often.'

The Schloss, which is still the seat of the House of Fürstenberg, underwent considerable restorations between 1892 and 1896. Although it is the family's private residence, it can be viewed by the public.

The Schloss overlooks its attractive, eighteenth century-style gardens, at the bottom of which are the banks of the River Brigach, a sizeable stream that flows through the town from the hills to the north west. About a kilometre downstream, it meets the River Breg, flowing from the south, underneath the main Donaueschingen north-to-south bypass. This is the point at which the Danube officially begins.

The Danube also officially begins in a small cluster of trees in the gardens of the Schloss. A folly in the form of a large, ornate well with a statue overlooking it, proclaims it as the spring which marks the actual source of the Danube.

With such an important river as the Danube, one would expect various versions of its official source, as historians, cartographers and local authorities agree to leave the matter romantically obscure!

On November 1st, the Mozarts were on the road once more, making for Munich. After an initially flat countryside, the coach soon entered Württemberg's wooded hills, along an attractive stretch of road, especially around Tuttlingen.

'Then,' wrote Leopold on November 10th, 'we made a headlong dash through Messkirch to Ulm. . . .'

It is likely that they put up once again at Zum Goldenen Rad, where they had spent a night on their outward journey.

Leopold, who prided himself on his discerning knowledge of architecture, did not like Ulm and had some disparaging comments to make about exposed timbers.

> 'Ulm is a horrid, old fashioned and tastelessly built place,' he wrote. 'Just picture to yourself houses in which the whole structure and wooden framework of the building and the way it is laid out have to show on the outside, and of which, after special effort has been made to

> beautify them, the framework is painted in colour, while the walls remain lovely and white; or in which every brick is painted in its natural colour so that the walls may be seen more clearly.'

Leopold went on to comment that Westerstetten, Geisingen, Göppingen, Plochingen and much of Stuttgart looked like that.

'. . . Günzburg. . .'

The historic centre of Günzburg is sheer delight; the long cobbled street running through the middle of the town has an archway at one end and a narrow entrance at the other. On either side stand typical Bavarian houses, many timber-framed and colourful.

'. . . and Dillingen, where we only stayed for two days, picked up two rings from the Prince. . . '

The Prince in question was the Prince-Bishop Joseph I of Augsburg, for whom the children gave a recital in the Schloss during their short stay.

Dillingen is a mediaeval fortress town. The Schloss was originally built in the twelfth century, and was the residence of the Prince-Bishops of Augsburg from the middle of the fifteenth century until 1803. From 1836 onwards it was reconstructed and altered many times, as it passed through a number of different tenancies, including local authorities. At the present time, it houses the town's Finance Department. The banqueting hall, the most likely room in which the concert took place, was radically altered in 1911, but some of the original features still remain, such as a marble fireplace framing a portrait of Bishop Clemenz Wenzeslaus above it.

Although there is no actual proof, the Mozarts almost certainly stayed at the posthotel Zum Goldenen Stern, where all visitors to the Prince-Bishop stayed. It has been rebuilt, and since 1958 the site has been where the Sparkässe bank now stands in the town centre, at the corner of the approach road to the Schloss.

The rings that were given to the children are in the Mozart Museum in Salzburg.

After Dillingen, the Mozarts travelled on to Biberbach.

The domain of Biberbach came into being in 1514

through its purchase by the House of Fugger, a wealthy and philanthropic catholic Augsburg family who did a tremendous amount of good both in their city and in the surrounding countryside. Shortly afterwards, an old crucifix with miracle-working properties was brought to the mediaeval church there, and Biberbach became a place of pilgrimage. The Parish and Pilgrimage Church of the Holy Cross, a breathtakingly beautiful example of baroque architecture, as well as a monastery, were built on the site of the original church. It was often referred to as the Fugger Church, in honour of its founder.

For the circumstance under which Wolferl played the organ of the Church of the Holy Cross in Biberbach, we may refer to some recollections in a letter, many years later, by one Pastor Christmann, who recalled some confusing circumstances surrounding the boyhood of one Father Sixtus Bachmann, Prior of Obermarchtal Monastery, on the Danube, from which the following story emerges:

When he was twelve years old, Sixtus Bachmann was studying at the Monastery at Biberbach, where he showed great aptitude on the organ. The young Bachmann's patron was Count Christoph Moritz Bernhard Fugger von Kircheim und Weissenborn. The latter had heard Wolfgang performing, and had persuaded the Mozarts to call at Biberbach on their way to Augsburg. Leopold readily agreed, and the Mozarts duly stopped at Biberbach on November 6th.

'The Count took particular advantage of the occasion,' wrote Pastor Christmann, 'when Herr Kappellmeister Mozart, then a young virtuoso travelling with his father, gave proof of his skills in music at the Count's castle. Young Bachmann was encouraged to enter into a contest with Mozart on the organ. Each did his utmost to dispute the other's advantage, and the competition ended very honourably for both.'

Or did it? Leopold made no mention of this occasion.

The organ on which the two boys sparred with their respective skills has been renovated: the casing in 1888 and the works themselves in 1972.

The same day, the Mozarts drove on to Augsburg.

'. . . and after spending a day in Augsburg . . .'

The Church of Holy Cross, Biberbach.
Source: Zaluski photograph.

According to a contemporary information leaflet dated November 13th, the Mozarts once more stayed at the Drei Mohren. Whether or not they called on family is not documented, but a month later, on December 11th, Leopold's mother died in Augsburg.

'. . . we came to Munich and are staying at Störzers. We arrived the day before yesterday.'

The post road from Donaueschingen followed the infant Danube, very broadly speaking, all the way to Dillingen, although today glimpses of the river are few and far between. Initially, it follows route 33 out of town; this very soon joins route 31 to Geisingen, where it becomes route 311 going on to Tuttlingen. It stays on route 311, leaving the Danube on the left, and continues through Messkirch, Herbertingen, Ehingen and all the way to Ulm.

The stretch between Geisingen and Mengen is a particularly attractive one, as it weaves through the thick, forested hills of Swabia. After Ulm, the post road becomes route 10 to Günzburg.

Günzburg had always been off the beaten track until the Empress Maria Theresia, in an effort to help the economic development of the town, re-routed the main Vienna to Paris post road to pass through it. It became a well-known and regular staging post, so it was also likely that the Mozarts stayed there. The post house at the time was 18 Augsburgerstrasse, and its stables were where the Gasthof zur Sonne stands at 32 Marktplatz. At the time that the Mozarts travelled here, the road had not been opened long. Most modern through roads are the old post routes, but as the centuries passed, this section of the road did not establish itself as the main through road from Ulm to Augsburg: today it is either route 10 or the autobahn. This accounts for the somewhat indirect, cross-country route between Ulm and Augsburg, especially the last section from Dillingen onwards.

Route 16 joins Günzburg and Dillingen. After Dillingen the road crosses the Danube in the direction of Holzheim and Augsburg and turns left towards Wertingen almost immediately after crossing the river. After Wertingen it makes for Gottmannshofen, Rieblingen and on to Biberbach. The church can be seen from afar, its steeple dominating the landscape.

From Biberbach the road goes on to Langweid am Lech, and joins route 2, which leads straight into Augsburg, and on to Munich.

SCENE SIX

Jottings on a Window-sill

The Mozarts arrived in Munich on Saturday, November 8th, and the following day they revisited the court of the Elector Maximillian III Joseph at Nymphenburg.

'Yesterday, Sunday,' wrote Leopold, 'we visited His Highness the Elector at table, and were graciously received. Wolfgang had to stand by the Elector and compose a piece of music; the Elector gave him the beginning or rather sang a few bars, and then he had to play it in the music room after dinner. You can imagine how surprised everyone was.'

Wolferl, as usual, excelled himself by being able to play the Elector's hummings instantly on the clavier, replete with accompaniment, and no doubt even managed to elaborate on it.

That night, Leopold noticed that Wolferl was not well. He was restless, and the following day Leopold decided to keep the boy in bed.

'With this weather and with the stove heating to which we now have to get used to, it is not surprising that such a fragile frame should suffer.'

In fact, Wolferl had been a little off-colour for several days, and it was now evident that he was again very ill. On the Monday his temperature rose considerably, and the following days saw the boy delirious and unable to stand. It is now generally accepted that Wolferl was suffering from rheumatic fever, with symptoms of weakness, abdominal pain, nosebleeds and weight loss.

A week later, Leopold wrote to Hagenauer again, recalling the time that the family returned from their first trip to Vienna (see 'Overture'):

> 'Our dear Frau Hagenauer will recall that Wolfgangerl became ill after our return from Vienna, and it was very bad, so that we feared it was smallpox. In the end it went to his feet and he complained at the pain. Now it is the same again. He cannot stand on his feet, or move his toes or knees; he would have nobody near him and for 4 nights he could not sleep. This took a lot out of him and we were very worried because all the time, particularly towards the evening, he was hot and feverish. He looks better today, but it will be a week before he is right again.'

By November 22nd Wolferl managed to get up, and seemed well enough to appear before the Elector once again. By any standards, it was a great error of judgment on Leopold's part to allow this.

Wolferl, despite being up and about, would have tired very easily, and any adult artist will readily confirm that performing anywhere, let alone in front of an eminent audience, is a physically and emotionally draining experience.

Besides, court etiquette forbade guests, courtiers and musicians from leaving before the Elector himself retired, which meant a late night for Wolferl at a time when he should have been convalescing. Rheumatic fever attacks the muscles of the heart, leaving permanent damage, and this was at least Wolferl's second attack of this disease. Leopold was playing a very dangerous game with his son's health in not allowing a full convalescence. The illness usually lasts a very long time, and has always been a major killer of children.

On top of this, everyone was forced to stand in the presence of the Elector, so Wolferl was even denied the luxury of resting his feet. We cannot judge how long it was before Wolferl was really well; Leopold is silent on this subject.

The 'present' from the Elector must have been given promptly, since the following day the Mozarts set off once again for home.

The post road from Augsburg to Munich is now route 2.

From Munich it follows route 304, which passes through Wasserburg, where the family stopped for the first few nights of the Grand Tour. Beyond Wasserburg lie Altenmarkt and Stein. Almost immediately after Stein a left turn leads into a minor road to Trauenreut, Waging and Freilassing, where it rejoins route 302 for the final short stretch over the Austrian border, and into Salzburg.

Leopold had intended taking the main Vienna post road out of Munich, as far as Altötting, and then turning south and following the River Salzach to Salzburg by way of Laufen.

However, the family spent the last few nights of their Grand Tour at the Seeon Monastery, which would have made a nonsense out of Leopold's original plan. It may well have been that because Wolferl was still not completely fit they took the shorter route.

The former Benedictine Monastery Church of St Lambert is beautifully situated on a tiny island on the Klostersee, a small lake a little way off to the south of the Salzburg post road. The whole monastic complex was founded in the tenth century, and exists to this day. Seeon can be reached by turning south either at Obing or at Rabenden, both of which lie between Wasserburg and Altenmarkt. The attractive lakeside town of Seeon is clearly signposted off the main road, as is the monastery itself, which is on the far side of the lake. The island is now joined to the mainland, and is easily accessible.

As usual, Leopold preferred to stay at a monastery, especially a Benedictine one, in preference to an inn. In the first instance, it was free, and he had personal contacts there, and in the second, there was every chance of Wolferl trying out the organ; also, being a devout catholic, he found it spiritually preferable.

Max Keller, the organist at the Court of Altötting, recounts how Wolferl by chance overheard a remark by the Prelate that they were lacking an Offertorium for the Feast of St Benedict on March 21st the following year. As a result, Wolferl slipped away from the supper table, installed himself on a nearby window-sill with pen and paper, and proceeded to write one for the Fathers. Hardly surprisingly, he did not manage to finish the work during the few days

The former Benedictine Monastery Church of St Lambert, Seeon, Bavaria.
Source: Załuski photograph.

that the family spent at Seeon; but he did sketch out a rough draft which he completed on his return to Salzburg.

The *Offertorium in Festo Sancti Benedicti: Scande coeli lumina, K34*, scored for four voices, two violins, bass, two trumpets, timpani and organ was duly presented to the Fathers in time for St Benedict's day the following Spring.

There is a commemorative plaque in the entrance to the monastery church, on the left.

The Mozarts returned in triumph to Salzburg on November 29th 1766, after an absence of just under three and a half years. True to custom, they were met on the post road by a whole host of their friends, led by the Hagenauers and Mme Robinig (with whom Nannerl was later to stay).

Leopold's fears that he would be in serious trouble with the Archbishop for having been away for so long were, in fact, unfounded. What was more, the Archbishop congratulated the whole family on their remarkable achievement in the greatest courts of Europe, pleased that the Archbishopric of Salzburg had basked in the reflected glory of the House of Mozart.

He was, however, sceptical about Wolferl's legendary prowess as a composer. He was convinced that his father helped him, as he had helped him in the past. Leopold had no objection to the Archbishop taking Wolferl, locking him in a room at the palace with pen and paper, and bidding him to compose. Always ready to oblige, Wolferl took up the challenge. After all, composing was his all-consuming passion, and his newly acquired skills were itching to create music. Deutsch records, for instance, that, 'he was often visited with musical ideas to which, even in the midst of the night, he would give utterance on his harpsicord.'

So Wolferl set about his labour with vigour, and by early the following year, he had written his first Oratorio, *Die Schuldigkeit des ersten Gebotes, K35*, scored for two sopranos, two tenors, two violins, two violas, bass, two flutes, two oboes, two bassoons, two horns and a trombone. Joseph Meissner, the travel-hungry singer who had been staying at Donaueschingen at the same time as the Mozarts only a few weeks previously, sang the part of Christianity at its premiere in Salzburg on March 12th 1767. Meissner was also to sing the part of Fracasso in Wolfgang's youthful opera *La finta semplice K51*, also in Salzburg on May 1st 1769.

Father Beda Hübner, a Benedictine monk of Salzburg who kept a diary, noted that:

> 'today the world famous Herr Leopold Mozart, the local vice-kappellmeister, with his family, two children, a boy of ten and a girl of thirteen, has arrived to the solace and joy of the whole city. It can well be that I have already elsewhere given an account of the Mozart family, especially since in the past 2 or 3 years nothing was written more often about in the newspapers than the wonderful art of the Mozart children. Both children, the boy as well as the girl, play the instrument, the harpsicord; the girl plays more artistically and is more than equal to her little brother, but the boy plays much more cleverly, and with well chosen ideas and with the loveliest touch, so that all, even excellent organists, are astounded that it can be humanly possible for such a boy of six to have been such an artist, and possess an art able to surprise the whole of the musical world. This Mozart family has been away from Salzburg almost 4 years by now, and has travelled over most parts of Europe.'

Even if Father Hübner got some of his figures wrong, he also mentioned that, 'Nannerl had become tolerably tall and almost marriageable,' and that, 'the boy Wolfgang has not grown much during this journey.'

But the last word of the Grand Tour must belong to Leopold Mozart, writing from Munich to Lorenz Hagenauer on November 10th, a letter which perhaps poses more questions than gives answers:

> 'God, who has been far too good to me, a miserable sinner, has given such talents to my children that, apart from my duty as a father, those talents alone would spur me on to sacrifice everything to their successful development. Every moment I lose is gone for ever. And if I at any time

guessed how precious time is for the young I realize it now. You know that my children are used to work. But if because of excuses they became used to hours of idleness, my whole plan would fall to the ground. Habit is an iron shirt. And you yourself know how much my children, especially Wolfgang, must learn. But who knows what they will do for us on our return to Salzburg? Perhaps what we shall encounter will make us only too glad to shoulder our bundles and clear out. But at least, God willing, I am going to bring my children back to their Fatherland. If they are not wanted it is not my fault, but people shall not get them for nothing.'

Children, or merchandise?

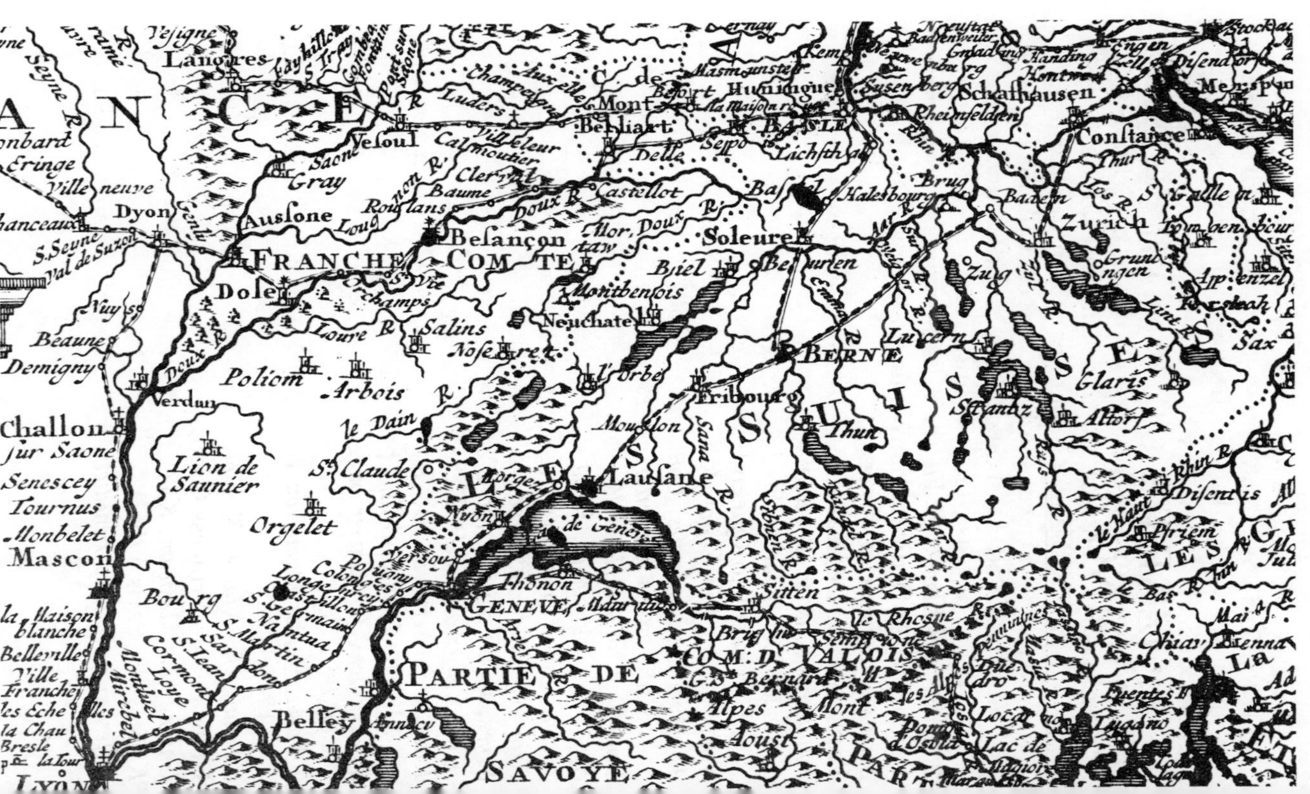
FRANCE
FRANCHE COMTE
PARTIE DE SAVOYE
COM. D. VALOIS
SUISSES
BERNE
Soleure
Basle
Huningue
Constance
Schafhausen
Rheinfelden
Zurich
Zug
Glaris
Altorf
Lucern
Fribourg
Thun
Lausanne
Morges
Nyon
Neuchatel
Biel
GENEVE
Thonon
Sitten
Besançon
Dole
Salins
Arbois
Poliom
Gray
Vesoul
Ausfone
Dyon
Beaune
Demigny
Verdun
Challon sur Saone
Senescey
Tournus
Monbelet
Mascon
Bourg
Belley
S. Claude
Orgelet
Lion de Saunier
Belliart
Delle
Langres
Lac de Geneve
Alpes
Mont
Aoust
Lac de Magiore
Locarno
Lugano
Fuentes
Chiavenna
Disentis
Sax
Appenzel
Belleville
Montluel
Mirebel
Loye
Cormont
S. Jean
Nantua
Castillon
Colonges
Versoy
Lyon

MOZART'S COMPOSITIONS DURING THE GRAND TOUR

2 Sonatas for Klavier & Violin, K6 & 7.
Paris 1763/4. Dedicated to Madame Victoire.
Sonata for Klavier & Violin, K8
Paris 1763/4. Dedicated to Comtesse de Tessé.
Sonata for Klavier & Violin, K9. Paris 1764.
6 Sonatas for Klavier & Violin/Flute (& Violincello), K10-15. Dedicated to Queen Charlotte.
Symphony No 1 in E flat, K16. London 1764/5.
42 Minuettos, Andantes, Contredanses, Rondos, Allemandes, Gigues, Sicilianos for klavier/organ, K15a-15ss. London 1764/5.
Symphony No 4 in D, K19. London 1765.
Sonata for four hands, K19d. (Unpublished).
Motet, God is our refuge, K20, London 1765.
Aria: Va dal furor portata, K21. London 1765.
Symphony No 5 in B flat, K22. The Hague 1765.
Aria: Conservati fedele, K23. The Hague 1765.
Klavier Concerto in D, K107 (arr. from 3 klavier sonatas by J.C.Bach). London/The Hague 1765.
8 Variations for klavier on Laat ons Juichen, K24. The Hague 1766.
7 Variations for klavier on Willem van Nassau, K25. Amsterdam 1766.
6 Sonatas for Klavier & Violin, K26-31.The Hague 1766.
Dedicated to Princess Caroline of Nassau-Weilburg.
Galimathias Musicum, K32. The Hague 1766.
Kyrie, K33. Paris 1766.
Offertorium in festo Benedicti, K34. Seeon/Salzburg 1766/7.

ACKNOWLEDGEMENTS

Gemeentearchief, Amsterdam.
Gemeentearchief, Antwerp.
Dr Mancal, Stadtarchiv Augsburg.
Dr Hans-Gunther Klein, Staatsbibliothek Preussicher Kulturbesitz.
Rev E O Williams, Barham Rectory, Canterbury.
Gerhild Schulze & Dr Hansmann, Stadtarchiv, Bonn.
Thomas Moos, Stadtarchiv, Bruchsal.
Leon Zylbergeld, Archives de la Ville de Bruxelles.
M Jacquette, Archives Municipales, Dijon.
Prof Klotzer, Stadtarchiv, Frankfurt.
Joris de Zutter, Stadsarchief, Ghent.
A Galletti of Bibliothèque Musicale, Genève.
Walther Grabert, Stadtarchiv, Günzburg.
C A J Bastiaenen, Gemeentearchief, den Haag.
Dr Theresia Zimmer, Landeshauptarchiv, Koblenz.
Frau M Wilkes, Historisches Archiv, Köln.
Walter Wastl, Bibliothek, Stiftsverwaltung, Lambach.
Pierre-Yves Favez, Archives Cantonales Vaudoises.
O Guffens & C de Vlies, Stadthuis Leuven.
D Balleriaux, Liège.
Dr Fritz Mayrhofer, Archiv Landeshauptstadt, Linz.
Herr Behr, Stadtarchiv, Ludwigsburg.
H Kruger, Schlossverwaltung, Ludwigsburg.
Mme Lise Florenne, Mozarteum de France, Lyon.
Prof Dr Chr.-H. Mahling, Johannes Gutenberg-Universität, Mainz.
Liselotte Homering, Stadt Reiss-Museum, Mannheim.
Cardinal Godfried Danneels, Aartsbisdom, Mechelen-Brussel.

Dr Fred Büttner, Munich University (Institute of Musicology).
Hubert Collin, Archives de Meurthe-et-Moselle.
Archives de Paris.
Herr Schaffner, Stadtarchiv, Passau.
Herr Dietz, Stadtverwaltung, Plochingen.
Iris Hartung, Leiterin des Stadtarchivs, Schwetzingen.
S Thomas & J Defau, Museum het Toreke, Tienen.
Marie-Pierre Dion, Bibliothèque Municipale, Valenciennes.
Peter Lennarts, Stadtarchiv, Brühl.
Roland Bossard, Musée Nationale des Châteaux de Versailles.
Bibliothèque Municipale, Versailles.
M François le Meignen, Archives Municipales de Versailles.
Dr U Helfenstein, Staatsarchiv des Kantons Zürich.
David Blake, The Hague.
Novello & Co Ltd, Music Publishers.